# Science in the Bible

Photograph by Harold M. Lambert, Philadelphia, Pa.

## Gaseous Nebula in Serpens

"The heavens declare his righteousness, and all the people see his glory" (Psalm 97:6).

# Science in the Bible

by

## Dr. Jean Sloat Morton

13 aug 18

MOODY PRESS
CHICAGO

# Acknowledgments

Grateful acknowledgment is made to the following, who have given editorial assistance: Dr. Merrill Cohen, MD.; Professor Willis Bishop, Washington Bible College; Mr. Norman Eberhard, World Weather; Dr. Homer Heater, Capitol Bible Seminary; Dr. David Johnson, Washington Bible College; Dr. Gerald Stover, Manna Bible Institute; Mrs. Virginia Workman, North Florida Christian School; and to my brother-in-law, the Reverend J. Arthur Sanders, Cumberland-Browns Presbyterian Church. Special thanks is extended to Mr. Alen Edgar, Graphics Arts Division of the Washington Bible College for many of the drawings. All drawings and photographs not acknowledged elsewhere in the book belong to the author.

© 1978 BY
THE MOODY BIBLE INSTITUTE
OF CHICAGO

Library of Congress Cataloging in Publication Data

Morton, Jean Sloat.
  Science in the Bible.

  Bibliography: p. 270
  SUMMARY: Discusses the numerous scriptural references to scientific subjects and examines their validity in the light of subsequent knowledge and discovery.
    1. Bible and science.  [1. Bible and science]
I. Title.
BS650.M67   220.8'5   77-17069
ISBN 0-8024-7629-5

Quotations from *The Amplified Bible,* copyright 1962, 1964 by Zondervan Publishing House, are used by permission.

Printed in the United States of America

# Contents

## Part III: CHEMISTRY

## Part IV: OCEANOGRAPHY

## Part V: EARTH SCIENCE

## Part VI: ZOOLOGY

## Part VII: BOTANY AND MICROBIOLOGY

# Foreword

Dr. Jean Morton's *Science in the Bible* will be an invaluable addition to the library of every Christian. It provides scientific documentation for the accuracy of the Bible at every point where the Bible interfaces with natural phenomena. Dr. Morton's training and experience in the science of biology, her study and love for the Word of God, her extensive research into all aspects of the subjects she covers in her book, and her use of many beautiful and accurate illustrations all combine to assure this book a place as a classic in its field. The average layman will find it fascinating reading, even if he has no scientific training. It may be used by instructors in Sunday school, Christian schools, and Christian colleges as a valuable sourcebook for insights into scientific topics touched on in the Bible.

Dr. Morton's book covers many aspects of astronomy, meteorology, chemistry, oceanography, earth science, botany, anatomy and physiology, genetics, and the medical sciences and health practices. While the Bible does not require scientific witness to its accuracy and divine authorship, that such a witness is available is made clear by Dr. Morton's exposition. Every Christian, every church library, and every Christian school should have a copy of this valuable and readable book.

DUANE T. GISH, PH.D.
Associate Director
Institute for Creation Research

# Introduction

The Bible is not primarily a book of science; it is a book of salvation, but wherever science is mentioned it is accurate. Many scientific facts, which prove the infallability of Scripture, are tucked away in its pages. These proofs are given in nonscientific language; nevertheless, they substantiate the claims of the authenticity of the Holy Scriptures. The channels of the sea, deep places of the ocean, and the sphericity of the earth are scientific phenomena recorded in Scripture ages before man discovered them.

This work was undertaken primarily to illustrate the numerous scriptural references to scientific subjects. In some cases, scientific concepts have been known through the ages, but these concepts are mentioned in a unique manner in Scripture. In other cases, scientific topics have been mentioned hundreds or even thousands of years before man discovered them. The so-called scientific errors of the Bible are frequently poetical statements, or they may be English translations that have lost their original meaning. The writer has attempted to explain some of these so-called errors.

It is hoped that this work will call your attention to the numerous scriptural references to scientific subjects. It is suggested that you, the reader, ponder just how the ancient writer could have acquired such scientific knowledge except through divine inspiration.

"For the prophecy came not in old time by the will of man: but holy men of God spake as they were moved by the Holy Ghost" (2 Peter 1:21).

Unless otherwise noted, the Scripture quotations are from the King James Version. The King James Version has been retained for its poetical beauty and ease of memorization. For simplicity of style and ease of reading, footnotes have been omitted.

# I

# ASTRONOMY

Photograph by Harold M. Lambert, Philadelphia, Pa.

## Spiral galaxy in ursa major

"The heavens declare the glory of God; and the firmament sheweth his handywork. Day unto day uttereth speech, and night unto night sheweth knowledge. There is no speech nor language, where their voice is not heard" (Psalm 19:1-3).

# 1

# Stars

Star names generally are derived from Greek or Latin; some are from Arabic. They have been named by astronomers, shepherds, desert nomads, and others. Johann Bayer (1603) devised a system of indicating the brightness, or magnitude, of stars. He utilized the Greek alphabet to denote their brightness, and, for further lettering, the Roman alphabet was used as needed. Thus, alpha Centauri is brighter than beta Centauri in the constellation Centauri.

The difference in brightness of the stars is indicated in 1 Corinthians 15:41, "One star differeth from another star in glory." The Greek for glory is *doxa* and is used to designate the divine light of God's presence. In this passage, the reference to stars seems to indicate their brightness or magnitude.

"In the beginning was the Word . . . And the Word was made flesh, and dwelt among us, (and we beheld his glory [doxa], the glory [doxa] as of the only begotten of the Father,) full of grace and truth" (John 1:1a, 14).

"There is one glory of the sun, and another glory of the moon, and another glory of the stars: for one star differeth from another star in glory" (1 Corinthians 15:41).

Various astronomers have estimated the number of stars. The estimates are incorrect and have increased throughout the years. Just for the sake of illustration, the following star data are used. There are at least $10^{11}$ number of galaxies, and each of these galaxies contains at least $10^{11}$ number of stars. The total number of stars is calculated by adding the exponents. This equals $10^{22}$ total number of stars. This is written as 10,000,000,000,000,000,000,000. In Genesis 15:5 Abraham was told to count the stars if he could. It is obvious from the analogy given to him of the sands of the sea that the stars cannot be numbered. According to the

13

## The stars photographed in space

"Lift up your eyes on high, and behold who hath created these things, that bringeth out their host by number: he calleth them all by names by the greatness of his might, for that he is strong in power; not one faileth" (Isaiah 40:26).

prophet Jeremiah, the host of heaven will never be numbered and heaven cannot be measured. "That in blessing I will bless thee, and in multiplying I will multiply thy seed as the stars of the heaven, and as the sand which is upon the seashore; and thy seed shall possess the gate of his enemies" (Genesis 22:17). "Thus saith the LORD ; If heaven above can be measured, and the foundations of the earth searched out beneath, I will also cast off all the seed of Israel for all that they have done, saith the LORD" (Jeremiah 31:37).

"As the host of heaven cannot be numbered, neither the sand of the sea measured: so will I multiply the seed of David my servant, and the Levites that minister unto me" (Jeremiah 33:22).

The height of the stars was totally unknown until the nineteenth century when Friedrich Wilhelm Bessel (1838) was able to compute distances of stars using the parallax method. Prior to that, astronomers had little knowledge about the height of stars. In the book of Job, Eliphaz has the right philosophy when he says: "Behold the height of the stars how high they are" (Job 22:12).

From these references, it is concluded that only the Lord is able to number the stars, calculate their precise distances, and name all of them. This is in accordance with what the Scripture says: "He telleth the number of the stars; he calleth them all by their names" (Psalm 147:4).

Photograph courtesy of Dack N. Patrick, Rockville, Md.

## Bethlehem

The Messiah's birth was predicted hundreds of years before it took place. It is not surprising that it would be heralded by a special star.

"But thou, Bethlehem Ephratah, though thou be little among the thousands of Judah, yet out of thee shall he come forth unto me that is to be ruler in Israel; whose goings forth have been from of old, from everlasting" (Micah 5:2).

"Now when Jesus was born in Bethlehem of Judea in the days of Herod the king, behold, there came wise men from the east to Jerusalem, saying, Where is he that is born King of the Jews? for we have seen his star in the east, and are come to worship him" (Matthew 2:1-2).

16

# 2

# The Star of Bethlehem

Some large planetariums have attempted to illustrate that the star of Bethlehem was a natural phenomenon. They give Christmas programs to demonstrate that the star was a nova, supernova, comet, or conjunction of planets. The known dates of such astronomical events do not agree with the birth of Christ, but even if they did, natural phenomena are not a plausible explanation of this miraculous event. If the idea of the conjunction of planets is accepted, numerous problems arise. For example, calculations show that the supposed event would not be overhead in Bethlehem. Furthermore, heavenly bodies do not appear, disappear, and then reappear; nor do they stand over a particular spot. The star of Bethlehem was a miracle comparable to the Shekinah glory that led the Israelites as a pillar of fire in the wilderness and stood over the tabernacle as a cloud.

The *Encyclopedia Judaica* defines *shekinah* as "dwelling" or "resting." It refers to the divine presence of the Lord. In rabbinical literature, the Shekinah Glory is associated with light. There are several references in the Old Testament that convey this idea. The Talmud also defines *shekinah* as "God's divine presence." Ezekiel 43:2 indicates that light is associated with the Shekinah glory, "The earth shined with his glory." A similar reference to the Shekinah glory is found in Exodus 3:2, "And the angel of Jehovah appeared unto him in a flame of fire out of the midst of a bush" (ASV).

Kittel's *Theological Dictionary of the New Testament,* in the etymology of the word *glory,* indicates that the Greek word *doxa* refers to the divine presence, or radiance that Moses saw in Exodus 33:9-23. The glory given to God is also shown in our word *doxology,* which is derived from *doxa.*

The reference to the star of Bethlehem in Matthew does not use the Greek word *doxa* in describing the star; however, it is used in Luke 2:9

17

where it describes the shepherds, "And the glory (Greek *doxa*) of the Lord shone round about them" (Luke 2:9).

The events in Matthew 2 and Luke 2 did not occur at the same time, but they are worthy of comparison. From the passage in Luke, it would seem the only plausible explanation of the star of Bethlehem is that it was a miraculous manifestation of God's glory. It is a miracle that cannot be explained by natural phenomena. Furthermore, the star of Bethlehem was not just any star, but it was called *His* star: "Now when Jesus was born in Bethlehem of Judea in the days of Herod the King, behold, there came wise men from the east to Jerusalem, saying, Where is he that is born King of the Jews? For we have seen his star in the east, and are come to worship him" (Matthew 2:1-2).

As pointed out above, the events in Matthew 2 and Luke 2 did not occur at the same time. In most all Christmas programs, however, the wise men and the shepherds visited the baby at the same time. Scripture does not support this view. The shepherds saw a "babe" in a manger (Luke 2:15-16). The wise men saw a "young child" in a house (Matthew 2:11).

# 3

# The Zodiacal Constellations

The Hebrew word *mazzaroth* is used in Job 38:32 to denote constellations. The derivation and significance of the Hebrew word are not understood, but from the context, constellations seem to be indicated. The twelve zodiacal constellations are brought forth in their seasons. As the earth moves around the sun in its yearly journey, it passes through the twelve zodiacal constellations. Each constellation makes its appearance for about a month at a time. Thus, they are brought forth in their seasons.

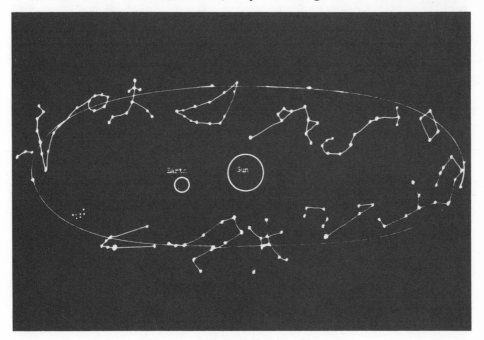

The zodiacal constellations

"Canst thou bring forth Mazzaroth in his season?" (Job 38:32).

The Pleiades

Job, "Canst thou bind the cluster of the Pleiades?" (Job 38:31*a*, ASV).

# 4

# The Pleiades

The Pleiades is an open cluster of stars commonly called the seven sisters. It is mentioned in Scripture under its Hebrew name *kimah*, which literally means "accumulation," or "heap." It is more closely related to the word *cluster*. There are at least two hundred stars that can be identified in the cluster from photographs. The *Larousse Encyclopedia of Astronomy* states that perhaps the cluster may have five hundred or more stars in all. Some stars are too weak to be photographed, and others may be in back of those being photographed. The cluster is named *pleiades* (seven) because of the seven stars which are supposed to be visible to the naked eye.

The phrase, "bind the cluster of the Pleiades" (Job 38:31, ASV) is sometimes interpreted to mean the dust clouds that surround certain members of the cluster. A better explanation of this phrase, however, seems to be the fact that the members of this cluster are physically associated, or bound into a cluster that is moving through space.

Only in recent years have photographic plates made it possible to identify true members of the cluster and distinguish them from other stars. Long before the advent of the telescope, God identified the cluster of the Pleiades as being bound together in a group. He asked Job if he could bind them together in a cluster. This is a highly scientific idea that man did not know until the stars were recorded by photographic plates.

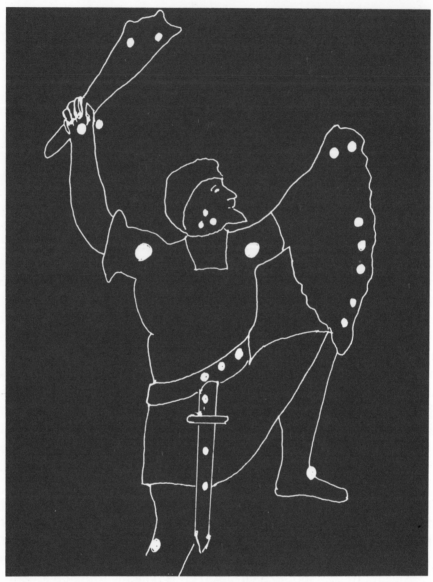

The constellation Orion

"Seek him that maketh the seven stars and Orion, and turneth the shadow of death into the morning, and maketh the day dark with night: that calleth for the waters of the sea, and poureth them out upon the face of the earth: the LORD is his name. . . . Which maketh Arcturus [the bear], Orion, and Pleiades, and the chambers of the south. Which doeth great things past finding out; yea, and wonders without number" (Amos 5:8; Job 9:9-10).

# 5

# Orion

The constellation Orion is mentioned in the Bible by the Hebrew name *kesil*, Job 9:9, Job 38:31, and Amos 5:8. The Targum of Jonathan refers to *kesil* as the giant; this most likely represents Orion, the mighty hunter. Abraham Ibn Ezra, who lived from 1092 to 1167, identified *kesil* as Orion in his commentary on Job. Ibn Ezra's identification of this term is very impressive, because he was an astronomer as well as a grammarian and Bible commentator. The plural *kesilim* in Isaiah 13:10 is best translated "constellations", as it is in the American Standard Version.

The question about Orion in Job 38:31 must be taken along with the question about the Pleiades, because the two appear to form an antithetical parallelism. Antithetical parallelisms are used in poetry to contrast opposite views such as good and evil, or wise and foolish. In this particular verse, the bound cluster of the Pleiades is contrasted with the unbound (loose) chains of stars in Orion. "Can you bind the cluster of the Pleiades, or loose the bands of Orion?" (Job 38:31, ASV).

The first star group, the Pleiades, is an open cluster that is bound together and moves through space together. The second group, Orion, is not bound. There is an association of stars in the sword, but they are not seen with the naked eye; they do not constitute the "chains" of stars in the constellation. To the observer, Orion appears as a group, but the stars are vast distances apart and unassociated. "The bands of Orion" refers to the chains of stars in the shoulders and legs that form a rectangle; the expression also applies to the chains in the belt, the lion skin, and the sword.

This astonishing truth was recorded in Scripture long before the telescope could differentiate these two groups as being bound and unbound.

## The Great Bear and the Little Bear

The most obvious configurations in the sky are the Big Dipper and the Little Dipper. Both dipper handles make up the tails of bears. Polaris, the North Star, is the last star in the handle of the Little Dipper. No doubt these stars were a familiar sight to Job. In Job's scientific examination, he is asked if he can guide the bear. "Canst thou guide the Bear with her train [sons]?" (Job 38:32*b*, ASV).

# 6

# The Great Bear—Ursa Major

The Great Bear constellation is known by a list of names such as Ursa Major, the Seven Brothers, and the Big Dipper. Although the Big Dipper is only a part of the constellation, it is sometimes used to identify the entire constellation. The Great Bear is mentioned under the Hebrew words *ash* and *ayish* found in Job 38:32 and Job 9:9. The Hebrew names are quite similar to the Arabic name *na'sh,* which means "a bier". The reference to guiding her train best describes the Great Bear constellation. "Her train" refers to the Little Bear, or Ursa Minor.

In his commentary on Job, Abraham Ibn Ezra (1092-1167) considered *ash* to be the Great Bear. *Ash,* or *ayish* in North Abyssinian folklore referred to the Seven Brothers, or the Big Dipper. It is also significant that the Great Bear is guided, because it moves around the pole (circumpolar); therefore, it is guided, not "led forth." Those constellations which are led forth generally appear every night for about one month in their turn, or during their season. The question put to Job has this concept: Job, can you lead forth the signs of the Zodiac in their seasons? Or can you guide the Bear with her sons (in a never ending circle around the north pole)?

In Job 9:9 and Job 38:32, the King James Version renders the Hebrew *ash* and *ayish* "Arcturus." The Hebrew words *ash* and *ayish* are best understood as the Great Bear constellation, as it is translated in the American Standard Version.

# 7

# Draco

Draco is a northern constellation made up of several stars that form the shape of a dragon. The Hebrew word is the same word translated *serpent* elsewhere. The constellation is generally called the dragon, or serpent. Draco moves around the pole in a never-ending circle. It is best seen in late spring or early summer. The star Thurban, located in this constellation, was once the North Star. It was by this star that the Egyptians oriented the great pyramids. In context, the reference in Job is to the heavens and to formation of the serpent, showing God's creative power.

Draco

"By his spirit he hath garnished the heavens; his hand hath formed the crooked serpent" (Job 26:13).

Photograph by Harold M. Lambert, Philadelphia, Pa.

## Halley's Comet, named for Edmund Halley

False prophets and apostate teachers are like wandering stars [comets] that are seen for only a short time. "Wandering stars, to whom is reserved the blackness of darkness for ever" (Jude 13).

# 8

# Comets

The word *comet* comes from the Latin *cometes,* which literally means "long-haired." The long hair refers to the trail of gases that streams out from a comet's tail. According to the latest theories, a comet is a group of rocky and metallic particles covered with frozen substances such as water, methane, carbon dioxide, ammonia, and various other gases. The comet is usually a few miles in diameter at its head. As it moves in its orbit toward the sun, the gases are vaporized, leaving a long-haired trail behind. As the comet moves away from the sun, the gases begin to freeze; the bright glow of the tail is gradually lost as it moves into the darkness of space. Photography shows that the comet completely loses the gaseous tail in total darkness.

Comets are not mentioned in Scripture by name, but there is a definite reference to them in Jude 13. They are called wandering stars and compared to false prophets, or apostate teachers. A comet is not a star like our sun; likewise, a false teacher is not a son of God. "They [false prophets] went out from us, but they were not of us; for if they had been of us, they would no doubt have continued with us: but they went out, that they might be made manifest that they were not all of us" (1 John 2:19).

A comet (false prophet) shines forth for only a short time, then it moves into the darkness of space. This is unlike true stars (sons) that continue to shine forth. "And they that be wise shall shine as the brightness of the firmament; and they that turn many to righteousness as the stars for ever and ever" (Daniel 12:3).

# 9

# The Sundial

"Every good and every perfect gift is from above, and cometh down from the Father of lights, with whom is no variableness, neither shadow of turning" (James 1:17).

The accompanying drawing is of an ancient sundial like some that have been found in Ephesus. Sundials were known since ancient times. They were common among the Hebrews, and the Bible records two miracles

Drawing by Alen Edgar, College Park, Md.

with regard to sundials (2 Kings 20:11; Isaiah 38:8). Sundials were common among the Chaldeans, Egyptians, Greeks, Chinese and Babylonians. Some historians maintain that they originated with the Babylonians.

In the book of James, the "shadow of turning" appears to make reference to a sundial. The classical interpretation of this verse is to attribute the shadow to an eclipse, but it seems more likely that it refers to a sundial. As the earth turns on its axis from west to east, a shadow is cast by turning.

The "shadow of turning" represents darkness and decay, which signify sin. The Lord is unchangeable; with Him there is no shadow of turning, no darkness or decay.

"God is light, and in him is no darkness at all" (1 John 1:5*b*).

# 10

# The Sun

The sun is an average star in a marvelous position to provide energy for planet earth. If the sun were closer, it would scorch the earth; if the sun were farther away, the earth would freeze. Not only is the sun the proper distance, but also the rate of the earth's rotation aids in the distribution of solar energy. Furthermore, the tilt of the earth distributes solar energy in such a way that it is one of the factors that cause the seasons. All these phenomena can be no mere accident; they must be the design of the Creator. Psalm 19:6 hints that the sun is the source of energy for the earth. It states that nothing is hid from the heat of the sun. Job indicates that the sun is the source of the wind systems upon the earth: "By what way is the light parted [distributed], which scattereth the east wind upon the earth?" (Job 38:24).

A marvelous scientific statement is found in Psalm 19:5-6 regarding the motion of the sun. Only recently has the sun's motion been identified. Prior to this, it was thought that the sun was fixed in space. In Psalm 19:5-6, the sun's motion is beautifully compared to a bridegroom coming out of his chamber, "His going forth is from the end of the heaven."

The sun is used as a picture of Christ the Son in Malachi 4:2. A similar statement is found in 2 Peter 1:19, where Christ is called the day star. The sun is the only star we see during the daytime.

"We have also a more sure word of prophecy; whereunto ye do well that ye take heed, as unto a light that shineth in a dark place, until the day dawn, and the day star arise in your hearts" (2 Peter 1:19).

# 11

# Light

Light has a dual nature; it may travel in waves or by energy packets known as photons. Photons are streaming particles of electric energy. Since light travels in a straight line, a shadow is produced by photons streaming past an object toward another surface. These paths of streaming photons are called light rays.

Job 38:19 asks where the way is where light dwells. The Hebrew word for "way" is *derek,* which means "trodden path." This implies motion. It is also significant that darkness dwells in a place (Job 38:19). The Hebrew word for "place" is *maqom. Maqom* means "place of standing" and implies the static nature of darkness. There are fewer and fewer photons as one moves from light into dim light, then into darkness. In total darkness there are no photons; it is static.

Until the seventeenth century, it was believed that light was transmitted instantaneously. Then Sir Isaac Newton suggested that light was composed of small particles which travel in a straight line. Christian Huygens proposed the wave theory of light. Olaus Roemer measured the velocity of light as evidenced by its delay as it traveled through space. In view of the findings of these scientists, it seems highly significant that Scripture suggests a path for light.

A beautiful analogy may be drawn from the fact that God is light. Light has a dual nature; Jesus had a dual nature—he was both human and divine. Light is frequently used in Scripture to represent truth or spiritual light. "Then spake Jesus again unto them, saying, I am the light of the world: he that followeth me shall not walk in darkness, but shall have the light of life" (John 8:12).

# 12

# Astrology and Other Forms of Divination

Astrology is a pseudo-science that seeks to chart the course of events and lives of individuals by observing the stars, planets, and other heavenly bodies. Astrology assigns to the stars power that rightfully belongs to God. Jeremiah 10:2 says not to be dismayed at the signs of the heaven; for the heathen are dismayed at them. Astrologers are condemned in Isaiah 47:13-14. In early Jewish writings both Leviticus 19:26 and Deuteronomy 18:10 were considered to oppose astrology.

The lights of the heavens are for the purpose of giving light and guidance. The star signs have been used for celestial navigation throughout the ages. Unfortunately, the signs of the zodiac have been misapplied in the pseudo-science of astrology.

A form of astrology, or star worship, was involved in the idol worship described in 2 Kings 17:16 and 23:4. Throwing kisses to heavenly bodies is mentioned in Job 31:26-28. All forms of magical arts and divination are forbidden in Scripture. In Acts 19:18-19, it is recorded that the Ephesians who practiced magical arts brought their books and burned them after they became believers. The monetary worth of the destroyed materials was said to be fifty thousand pieces of silver, possibly $10,000.

Three forms of divination are mentioned in Ezekiel 21:21. When the king of Babylon came to the forks of the road, he used divination to determine which fork he would take. He wanted to decide whether to proceed against Jerusalem, the capital of Judah or against the Ammonites at Rabbath. The first form of divination was to shoot an arrow and see whether it went to the left side or to the right side of the road. This determined which fork of the road he would take. He also inquired of images, possibly Teraphim. Next, he looked into the liver, which method is similar to looking into tea leaves or the palm of the hand. It was customary to kill a chicken and examine the liver; the veins of the liver are supposed to suggest the path to take. If a live chicken was not available, clay models of a liver were sometimes used.

Several writers have suggested that the signs of the zodiac represent the redeemer, such as the Lion of the Tribe of Judah. (See the *Witness of the Stars* by Bullinger).

"Thus saith the LORD . . . That frustrateth the tokens of the liars, and maketh diviners mad; that turneth wise men backward, and maketh their knowledge foolish; . . . Let now the astrologers, the stargazers, the monthly prognosticators, stand up, and save thee from these things that shall come upon thee. Behold they shall be as stubble; the fire shall burn them; they shall not deliver themselves from the power of the flame" (Isaiah 44:24-25, 47:13-14).

# 13

# Saturn

Saturn is the sixth planet from the sun. It is referred to in Amos 5:25-26 under the name of *Chiun,* and it was the object of idol worship. The word *Chiun* from the Old Testament is thought to be derived from the Assyrian *Kaiwanu,* the name of Ninib, god of the planet Saturn. The planet is referred to in the book of Acts by the term *Remphan.* The derivation of the word is not clear, but perhaps it is an Egyptian dialectic word for Saturn. When Stephen quoted Acts 7:43, he was quoting from the Septuagint, which renders the word "Remphan."

> Have ye offered unto me sacrifices and offerings in the wilderness forty years, O house of Israel? But ye have born the tabernacle of your Moloch and Chiun your images, the star of your god, which ye made to yourselves (Amos 5:25-26).

> Yea, ye took up the tabernacle of Moloch, and the star of your god Remphan, figures which ye made to worship them: and I will carry you away beyond Babylon (Acts 7:43).

Both Moloch and Chiun are associated with stellar deities. It is not clear, however, which star is represented by Moloch. Some authorities say Chiun and Moloch are both related to the planet Saturn. It seems more likely that Moloch worship was associated with the constellation Tarus, the bull. The golden calf may have represented this constellation. Although the exact stellar counterpart of Moloch cannot be identified, one thing is certain; it involved the sacrificing of children by passing them through the fire. This form of worship is mentioned along with calf worship in the Old Testament. "And they left all the commandments of the LORD their God, and made them molten images, even two calves, and made a grove, and worshipped all the host of heaven, and served Baal. And they caused their sons and their daughters to pass through the fire, and used divination and enchantments, and sold themselves to do evil in the sight of the LORD, to provoke him to anger" (2 Kings 17:16-17).

Photograph by Wolfe Worldwide Films, Los Angeles, Calif.

## Sunset over the Nile

From the rising of the sun unto the going down of the same the Lord's name is to be praised (Psalm 113:3).

Photograph by Harold M. Lambert, Philadelphia, Pa.

## Photons (rays of light) streaming through trees

"The entrance of thy words giveth light; it giveth understanding unto the simple" (Psalm 119:130).

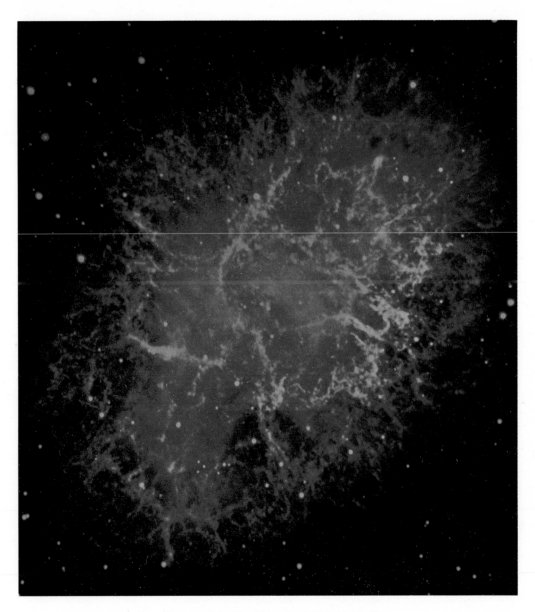

Photograph by Harold Lambert, Philadelphia, Pa.

## The Crab Nebula

"And beware lest you lift up your eyes to the heavens, and when you see the sun, moon, and stars, even all the host of the heavens, you be drawn away and worship them and serve them, things which the Lord your God has allotted to all nations under the whole heavens" (Deuteronomy 4:19, Amplified Bible).

Photograph by Harold M. Lambert, Philadelphia, Pa.

## Saturn

The planet Saturn was worshipped in the Old Testament under the name of *Chiun* and in the New Testament under the name of *Remphan.*

"Thou shalt not make unto thee any graven image, or any likeness of any thing that is in heaven above, or that is in the earth beneath, or that is in the water under the earth" (Exodus 20:4).

# 14

## Venus

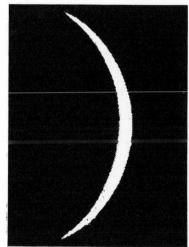

Venus

"I Jesus have sent mine angel to testify unto you these things in the churches. I am the root and the offspring of David, and the bright and morning star" (Revelation 22:16).

Venus is generally known as the morning star, although other planets may appear as the bright star of the morning. In Revelation 22:16, Christ is called the bright and morning star.

Most heathen gods have an astronomical counterpart or are assigned some magical power over a heavenly body. These gods are often supposed to have some particular power over a planet or star. The belief in powers of false gods over astronomical bodies is idolatry. It delegates to false gods power that rightfully belongs to Christ.

It was common practice in ancient times, especially among the Assyrians and Babylonians, to recognize stellar deities for their gods. The Babylonians Ishtar, known as the Queen of heaven, was supposed to be linked to the planet Venus. Judean women were fond of this heathen goddess; they made drinks and cake offerings to her (Jeremiah 7:18; 44:17-19). The cakes were known as the bread of Ishtar. Ishtar was represented by the planet Venus. Venus is often seen drawn as a star on various objects that have been excavated.

"The children gather wood, and the fathers kindle the fire, and the women knead their dough, to make cakes to the queen of heaven, and to pour out drink-offerings unto other gods, that they may provoke me to anger" (Jeremiah 7:18).

# 15

# Meteors

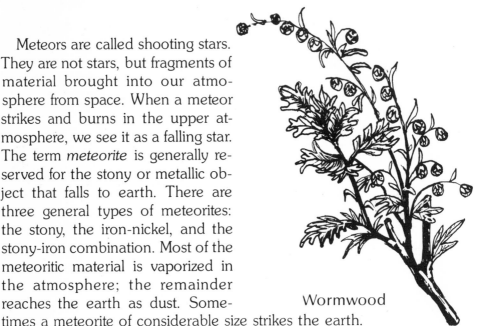

Wormwood

Meteors are called shooting stars. They are not stars, but fragments of material brought into our atmosphere from space. When a meteor strikes and burns in the upper atmosphere, we see it as a falling star. The term *meteorite* is generally reserved for the stony or metallic object that falls to earth. There are three general types of meteorites: the stony, the iron-nickel, and the stony-iron combination. Most of the meteoritic material is vaporized in the atmosphere; the remainder reaches the earth as dust. Sometimes a meteorite of considerable size strikes the earth.

Several references to falling stars or meteorites are made in Scripture. The book of Revelation speaks of a meteorite that will pollute the waters: "And there fell a great star from heaven, burning as it were a lamp. . . . And the name of the star is called Wormwood: and the third part of the waters became wormwood; and many men died of the waters, because they were made bitter" (Revelation 8:10*b*-11).

This comparison to wormwood is unusual. Wormwood is a plant that is similar to the American sagebrush in appearance. Small amounts of an extract of the plant are used to make a drink. It is added to alcohol and quite popular in France. The plant is extremely bitter and contains absinthe. Absinthe is very toxic in large amounts, and prolonged use causes mental deterioration, insanity, and finally death.

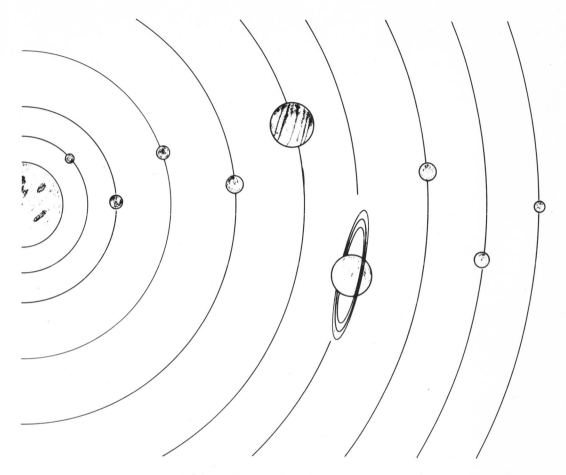

## The ordinances of heaven

God has established certain physical laws that control the movement of the stars and planets in their orbits. These laws are in force night and day as the earth rotates. The permanence of these laws is seen from the fact that while the earth remains, day and night shall not cease (Genesis 8:22). God used the permanence of day and night (Jeremiah 33:20) and the moon as a faithful witness in the sky, (Psalm 89:34-37) as illustrations of the permanence of His covenant with David. God's promise that the Messiah would sit on the throne of David is sure, as sure as the sun and moon and stars which move in their orbits.

My covenant will I not break, nor alter the thing that is gone out of my lips. Once have I sworn by my holiness that I will not lie unto David. His seed shall endure for ever, and his throne as the sun before me. It shall be established for ever as the moon, and as a faithful witness in heaven. Selah. (Psalm 89:34-37).

41

# 16

# The Ordinances of Heaven

The phrase "the ordinances of heaven" refers to the physical laws that govern celestial bodies. The movement of the planets, stars, and constellations are governed by these laws. The planets, stars, and constellations are a faithful witness in the sky. Considering the billions of celestial bodies in space, nothing is as precise as their motion. The permanence and precision of these physical laws are seen in Jeremiah 31:35-36, where these laws are compared to the permanence of God's covenant with Israel.

> Thus saith the LORD, which giveth the sun for a light by day, and the ordinances of the moon and of the stars for a light by night, which divideth the sea when the waves thereof roar; the LORD of hosts is his name. If those ordinances depart from before me, saith the LORD, then the seed of Israel also shall cease from being a nation before me for ever (Jeremiah 31:35-36).

One of the scientific questions asked Job was if he knew the ordinances of heaven (Job 38:33). The ordinances of the moon and stars, as referred to in Jeremiah 33:25, indicate their regular appearance in their orbits. Consistent orbital movement brings about the regular phases of the moon. As sure as the moon goes through its phases, and as sure as the sun and stars shine, so God's covenant is sure to be fulfilled.

Heavenly bodies do not follow the rule of chance. They follow the physical laws designed by the Creator. Day after day heavenly bodies move in their orbits, as if the heavens were speaking and declaring aloud the glory of the Creator. The psalmist has so aptly described their daily precision in Psalm 19:1-3: "The heavens declare the glory of God; and the firmament showeth his handiwork. Day unto day uttereth speech, and night unto night sheweth knowledge. There is no speech nor language, where their voice is not heard."

### The moon

Praise ye the LORD. Praise ye him, sun and moon: praise him, all ye stars of light. Praise him, ye heavens of heavens, and ye waters that be above the heavens. Let them praise the name of the LORD; for he commanded, and they were created. He hath also established them forever and ever: he hath made a decree which shall not pass (Psalm 148:1a, 3-6).

# 17

# The Moon

The Hebrews use the twenty-eight day lunar cycle to calculate their months of the year. In most references, the use of the words *new moon* means the first of the month. The phrase "new moon to new moon" generally means "monthly." Deuteronomy 33:14 is often said to be a superstitious belief held by the Hebrews that the moon caused plants to grow. A careful analysis of the verse indicates that it actually refers to the monthly yield. This verse is speaking of the blessing of the abundant monthly yield of fruits and vegetables. The verse does not have anything to do with superstition.

The moonlight was extremely important for traveling at night by camel caravans. It is still honored in modern times by the bedouins, who make moon shaped crescents for their camels' gear. The moonlight was essential for traveling during the cool part of the night. The bedouins traveled at night to avoid the scorching sun. The phrase, "The sun shall not smite thee by day, nor the moon by night" (Psalm 121:6), refers to God's loving care throughout the day and night.

The "ordinances of the moon" in Jeremiah 31:35 refer to the moon's phases. The moon remains in its orbit and brings forth its phases with such constancy that it compares to God's faithfulness to Israel. The moon was said to be given for seasons in Psalm 104:19-23. This refers to the lunar calendar of Israel. Twelve lunar months were recognized by the Hebrews as a year. "And Solomon had twelve officers over all Israel, which provided victuals for the king and his household: each man his month in a year made provisions" (1 Kings 4:7).

# 18

# Heaven Is Northward

There are three heavens mentioned in Scripture. The apostle Paul said he was caught up to the third heaven (2 Corinthians 12:2). The first heaven is the atmosphere where the birds fly (Jeremiah 8:7). The second heaven is where the celestial bodies are located (Genesis 1:14-17). The third heaven is God's heaven, and its location is indicated as northward; "And if his offering be of the flocks, namely, of the sheep, or of the goats, for a burnt-sacrifice; he shall bring it a male without blemish. And he shall kill it on the side of the altar northward before the LORD" (Leviticus 1:10-11). Satan recognized the importance of the north: "How art thou fallen from heaven, O Lucifer. . . . For thou hast said in thine heart, I will ascend into heaven, I will exalt my throne above the stars of God: I will sit also upon the mount of the congregation, *in the sides of the north*" (Isaiah 14:12*a*, 13; italics added).

It is highly significant that the north is omitted from Psalm 75:6. It implies that promotion comes from the north. "For promotion cometh neither from the east, nor from the west, nor from the south. But God is the judge; he putteth down one, and setteth up another" (Psalm 75:6-7).

Photograph by Harold M. Lambert, Philadelphia, Pa.

Hath the rain a father,
Or who hath begotten the drops of dew?
Out of whose womb came the ice?
And the hoary frost of heaven, who hath gendered it?

Who hath ascended up into heaven, or descended?
Who hath gathered the wind in his fists?
Who hath bound the waters in a garment?
Who hath established all the ends of the earth?
What is his name and what is his son's name,
If thou canst tell? (Job 38:28-29; Proverbs 30:4).

# II

# METEOROLOGY AND CLIMATOLOGY

Drawing by Alen Edgar, College Park, Md.

## The hydrologic, or water, cycle

"All the rivers run into the sea; yet the sea is not full; unto the place from whence the rivers come, thither they return again" (Ecclesiastes 1:7).

# 19

# The Hydrologic, or Water, Cycle

The water cycle consists of three major phases: evaporation, condensation, and precipitation. Solar heat causes millions of tons of water to evaporate daily from the oceans and other streams. Bodies of water send a steady stream of water vapor into the air; plants transpire water vapor and add to this steady stream. One average size tree may transpire four or five thousand gallons of water vapor per year. The vapor ascends into the air, but whenever the air is cooled below the saturation point, the vapor condenses to form clouds. When the clouds are full, droplets unite to form rain. "If the clouds be full of rain, they empty themselves upon the earth" (Ecclesiastes 11:3a).

When precipitation occurs, part of the water is stored as ground water, and some is utilized by plants. The balance runs off to lakes, ponds, rivers, and oceans; then the cycle repeats itself. Note that the sea is the source of rain. "He . . . calleth for the waters of the sea, and poureth them out upon the face of the earth: the LORD is his name" (Amos 9:6b).

The idea of a complete water cycle was not generally accepted until the sixteenth and seventeenth centuries. The first substantial evidence on the cycle came from experiments of Pierre Perrault and Edme Mariotte. These scientists demonstrated that the flow of the Seine River could be accounted for by precipitation. Astronomer Edmund Halley also contributed valuable data to the concept of a complete water cycle. He demonstrated that precipitation and evaporation balanced one another. These scientists established the idea of a complete water cycle. More than two thousand years before their discovery, the Scripture indicated a water cycle in Ecclesiastes 1:7: "From whence the rivers come, thither they return again." (Compare Psalm 135:7 and Jeremiah 10:13.)

Photograph by Harold M. Lambert, Philadelphia, Pa.

## The product of God's goodness

"Sing unto the LORD with thanksgiving; sing praise upon the harp unto our God: who covereth the heaven with clouds, who prepareth rain for the earth, who maketh grass to grow upon the mountains" (Psalm 147:7-8).

# 20

# Ground Water

Whenever rain falls on land, some of it runs off to lakes, rivers, and eventually to the oceans. Part of the water does not run off but is kept as ground water. The surface soils can hold some of the rain; the balance seeps down into cracks and crevices of the earth.

Most of the surface moisture is available to plants, but a great deal of it goes too deep into the ground to be utilized by some plants. In arid countries, such as parts of the Middle East, ground water is absorbed by plants with long root systems that are able to bring up water to the surface. These plants are called *phreatophytes,* meaning well plants. Salt grasses and certain types of palms are examples of well plants.

Prior to the work of Pierre Perrault and Edme Mariotte, it was thought that ground water could not be derived from precipitation. It was generally assumed that the earth was impenetrable and would not allow rainwater to go beneath the surface. The work of these two scientists showed that ground water was derived mainly from precipitation. (Reported in *The Book of Popular Science,* Vol. 8, page 321, 1969).

As previously mentioned, the Scripture indicates there is a water cycle because it says, "from whence the rivers come, thither they return again," (Ecclesiastes 1:7). Not all the water from precipitation enters the water cycle immediately, but part of it serves as ground water. Ages before the work of Pierre Perrault and Edme Mariotte, the Scripture indicated that precipitation was the source of ground water. "For as the rain cometh down, and the snow from heaven, and returneth not thither, but watereth the earth, and maketh it bring forth and bud, that it may give seed to the sower, and bread to the eater" (Isaiah 55:10).

Photograph by Harold M. Lambert, Philadelphia, Pa.

## Rain clouds

God's blessings upon his people include the gentle rains, both the former and the latter.

"Be glad then, ye children of Zion, and rejoice in the LORD your God: for he hath given you the former rain moderately, and he will cause to come down for you the rain, the former rain, and the latter rain in the first month. And the floors shall be full of wheat, and the vats shall overflow with wine and oil" (Joel 2:23-24).

# 21

# The Former and Latter Rains

"For there is a sound of abundance of rain" (1 Kings 18:41*b*).

Rain is very precious in a hot, dry climate such as Palestine. There are three rainy periods: the former rains, the winter rainy season, and the latter rains. The former rains follow a hot dry summer and begin in late September or early October. Sometimes the rains may be delayed until very late fall. The winter is a rainy season during the months of December and January. The problem is not so much the total amount of rainfall but the fact that torrents of rain continue to fall in a short period of time. Although the Palestinians appreciate the rain, continuous rain can eventually become tiresome. "A continual dropping in a very rainy day and a contentious woman are alike" (Proverbs 27:15).

The latter rains occur around March and April. This rain is essential for harvest because it helps bring about the swelling of the fruit at a time during its critical development. The former and the latter rains are necessary to insure a good harvest. "And it shall come to pass, if ye shall hearken diligently unto my commandments which I command you this day, to love the LORD your God, and to serve him with all your heart and with all your soul, that I will give you the rain of your land in his due season, the first rain and the latter rain, that thou mayest gather in thy corn, and thy wine, and thine oil" (Deuteronomy 11:13-14).

The withholding of rain was a sign of God's displeasure. In Amos 4:6-7, God withheld the rain three months before harvest and caused a famine. The Israelites had clean teeth because there was no food in them.

# 22

# Waterspouts

A waterspout is like a tornado in some respects. Tornadoes occur over land, but waterspouts occur over bodies of water. There are other differences between tornadoes and waterspouts. Tornadoes are generally more violent than waterspouts, although spouts may occasionally become violent. Captain Holmes, in *Weather Made Clear,* reports that waterspouts may travel clockwise or counterclockwise as compared to tornadoes, which always travel counterclockwise in this hemisphere.

Spouts form as a funnel from the base of a cumulus or cumulonimbus cloud. As the cloud projects downward, the sea forms a whirling disturbance known as an eddy. The sea lifts upward as though it were pushed from below. Saltwater may be drawn upward from the ocean as sky and ocean seem to meet.

Most waterspouts are relatively mild and are composed chiefly of fine spray. These amount to nothing more than a fine mist when they are encountered. If a violent waterspout occurs, it makes an enormous roar. The violent waterspout may bring disaster to a seagoing vessel. Modern ships are able to move out of a waterspout's path, so it does not pose any serious threat.

Strong waterspouts may form two tubes; a funnel outside, formed by a low pressure system causing the cloud projection, and an inner tube of water, pulled up by a near vacuum. This may cause seawater to be drawn upward and later fall as salty rain. In 1895, a large waterspout developed over Vineyard Sound, Massachusetts. Saltwater was carried aloft, and hours later fish and saltwater fell on Martha's Vineyard. (Reported by Captain D. C. Holmes, U.S.N. in *Weather Made Clear*, New York: Sterling, 1965.)

Psalm 42:7 describes a waterspout. In this verse the description is used in a comparative sense; nevertheless, it contains a scientific truth. The psalmist has the violent type of waterspout in mind. The roaring sound is echoed in the deep as the vacuum* pulls up the sea water. God said this centuries before man knew that saltwater was drawn up in a waterspout. The wording in this verse: "Deep calleth unto deep," might imply that animals are communicating at this roaring. Until recently it was thought that marine life could not exist at great depths. Recent deep sea data indicate that sea life is found at all depths. In this verse the use of the Hebrew *tehom* refers to abyssal depth. The Hebrew text actually reads: "*Tehom* calleth unto *tehom*."

Drawing by Alen Edgar, College Park, Md.

## A waterspout

"Deep calleth unto deep at the noise of thy waterspouts" (Psalm 42:7).

*Vacuum defined here as pressure difference between inside and out.

Photograph by Harold M. Lambert, Philadelphia, Pa.

## Storm at sea

"Thou rulest the raging of the sea: when the waves thereof arise, thou stillest them" (Psalm 89:9).

# 23

# God's Power in Nature

Storms are conditions of violent atmospheric disturbance. They are centers of massive power, and a tremendous amount of energy is released in each storm. A single hurricane may export as much as 3,500,000,000 tons of air, with wind speeds of 100-200 miles an hour and a total force of $6 \times 10^{25}$ ergs per second of power.

God's power is revealed in these storms, according to Psalm 107:23-31:

They that go down to the sea in ships, that do business in great waters; these see the works of the LORD and his wonders in the deep. For he commandeth, and raiseth the stormy wind, which lifteth up the waves thereof. They mount up to the heaven; they go down again to the depths: their soul is melted because of trouble. They reel to and fro, and stagger like a drunken man, and are at their wits' end. Then they cry unto the LORD in their trouble, and he bringeth them out of their distresses. He maketh the storm a calm, so that the waves thereof are still. Then are they glad because they are quiet; so he bringeth them unto their desired haven. Oh, that men would praise the LORD for his goodness, and for his wonderful works to the children of men!

The power and majesty of the Lord are further revealed in the calming of a storm as recorded in the Gospels. "And he [Jesus] arose, and rebuked the wind, and said unto the sea, Peace, be still. And the wind ceased, and there was a great calm. . . . And they feared exceedingly, and said one to another, What manner of man is this, that even the wind and the sea obey him?" (Mark 4:39, 41).

Photograph courtesy of National Oceanic and Atmospheric Administration, Rockville, Md.

## Hurricane

"The Lord hath his way in the whirlwind and in the storm, and the clouds are the dust of his feet" (Nahum 1:3b).

58

Photograph from *Snow Crystals* by W. A. Bentley and W. J. Humphreys, Dover Publications.

## Snow crystals

"Come now, and let us reason together, saith the LORD: though your sins be as scarlet, they shall be as white as snow; though they be red like crimson, they shall be as wool" (Isaiah 1:18).

# 24

# Snow

Water vapor in a cloud crystallizes to form snow if the temperature of the cloud is below freezing. If the temperature between the cloud and ground is much above freezing, the snow melts and falls as rain. Snow is formed directly from vapor and should not be confused with sleet. Sleet is frozen rain.

Nothing in nature shows forth the Lord's handiwork so much as the intricate pattern of snow crystals. Experimental evidence indicates that when water freezes, the atoms of the ice crystals are connected together in a pattern of hexagons. Snow crystals also display this consistent hexagonal pattern. If you examine snow crystals all day long with a strong magnifier, no two crystals will ever be exactly alike. Surely this intricate pattern of snow crystals bears evidence of design by the Designer.

Snow is mentioned in the Bible with reference to the purity and righteousness of the believer in Isaiah 1:18 and in Psalm 51:7: "Purge me with hyssop, and I shall be clean: wash me, and I shall be whiter than snow."

Snow is mentioned in the Bible as being a treasure reserved for war. Both hail and snow have been used in judgment. In some instances hail and snow have been decisive factors in war. Snow played an important role in Napoleon's defeat. "Hast thou entered into the treasures of the snow? Or hast thou seen the treasures of the hail, which I have reserved against the time of trouble, against the day of battle and war?" (Job 38:22-23).

## Mount Hermon

"Behold, how good and how pleasant it is for brethren to dwell together in unity! It is like the precious ointment upon the head, that ran down upon the beard, even Aaron's beard: that went down to the skirts of his garments; as the dew of Hermon, and as the dew that descended upon the mountains of Zion: for there the LORD commanded the blessing, even life for evermore" (Psalm 133).

# 25

# Dew

Warm air will hold more moisture than cool air, but if warm, moist air is cooled, it reaches a point where it is saturated and the excess vapor begins to condense. The temperature at which condensation begins to occur is known as the dew point. Dew is water vapor that has condensed on objects and surfaces.

Dew is very important in Palestine, particularly at harvest time. It is necessary for the swelling of the fruits. Dew is considered a mark of blessing and prosperity. When Isaac blessed Jacob he said, "Therefore God give thee the dew of heaven" (Genesis 27:28). It was also a mark of blessing to the tribes of Israel. Of Joseph Moses said, "Blessed of the LORD be his land, for the precious things of heaven, for the dew" (Deuteronomy 33:13). Dew was associated with Job's prosperity, "And dew all night on my branches" (Job 29:19). (See also the miracle of the dew on the fleece, Judges 6:36-40.)

Dew is frequently used in a comparative sense because it goes away early (Hosea 6:4; 13:3). In Psalm 133, brotherly love is compared to the life-giving dew of Mount Hermon. The dew is of great benefit in a dry country; likewise, unity of the brethren is of great benefit.

Photograph courtesy of National Weather Service, National Oceanic and Atmospheric Administration, Rockville, Md.

## Fair-weather cumulus clouds

Fair-weather cumulus clouds are white, puffy clouds without rain. They are like those described in the following verses. "Whoso boasteth himself of a false gift is like clouds and wind without rain" (Proverbs 25:14). "There are spots in your feasts of charity, when they feast with you, feeding themselves without fear: clouds they are without water, carried about of winds; trees whose fruit withereth, without fruit, twice dead, plucked up by the roots" (Jude 12).

# 26

# Fair-Weather Cumulus Clouds

Fair-weather cumulus clouds are small, white, puffy clouds that resemble balls of cotton. Cumulus clouds usually form over land areas as the warm air rises during the daytime. As a rule, fair-weather clouds disappear at night. They generally represent good weather, but may pile up to form cumulonimbus storm clouds.

In the book of Proverbs, cumulus clouds are compared to a boaster because cumulus cloud droplets are not large enough to form rain. Since the moisture content is not adequate for rain, they are fake, or what we might term "bags of wind." Here the comparison of a boaster to a windbag seems most appropriate. The common Hebrew term for cloud is *anan*, and the common term for thick cloud is *ab*. Neither of these words is used in Proverbs 25:14. Instead, the Hebrew word *nasi* is used to describe a cloud which is exalted, or lifted up. This signifies the nature of the boaster who exalts himself.

In Jude 12, cumulus clouds are again referred to as waterless clouds. Fair-weather cumulus clouds do not generally cause a problem, but they can pile up to form storm clouds. Likewise, a boaster or windbag may sometimes create a real problem.

The Bible says fair weather clouds are waterless. This is indeed a scientific statement for the time that it was written.

# 27

# The Wisdom of God
# as Revealed in the Clouds

Job 38:36 has been translated in numerous ways, but most of the translations do not agree with the context. The information that precedes and follows Job 38:36 should be considered to make an accurate translation. "Canst thou lift up thy voice to the clouds, that abundance of waters may cover thee? Canst thou send lightnings, that they may go, and say unto thee, Here we are? Who hath put wisdom in the inward parts? or who hath given understanding to the heart? Who can number the clouds in wisdom? or who can stay the bottles of heaven?" (Job 38:34-37).

It becomes obvious from the context that verse 36 must refer to weather phenomena, such as the clouds. There are some cases in Scripture where thoughts are interjected for comparison or illustration, but that does not seem to be the case here. The verse does not deal with physiology, the inward parts of man, or the heart. Furthermore, it does not deal with the intellectual endowments of man. In context, the verse deals with weather phenomena such as clouds, lightning, and rain.

Job was asked if he could command the rain (v. 34). Verse 35 indicates that "the lightnings" obey God's command. "The lightnings" are personified to denote their obedience to God. They answer, "here we are," or, more literally, "behold us." The word translated "inward parts" (v. 36) is the Hebrew word *tuchoth* from the root word for "covered over." The verb *tuach* used in Ezekiel 22:28 means "to daub over," or "overlay." In context, it refers to cloud layers. Thus, the first phrase of the verse might be translated: "Who put wisdom in the cloud layers?"

The word *heart* in verse 36b is not the word usually translated *heart*. The Hebrew word is *sekvi*, which comes from a root word meaning "to look upon," or "to view." The noun could be translated "that which is viewed" or "an object looked upon," such as weather phenomena or cloud formations. In this sense it most likely refers to cloud formations. The verse must refer to weather phenomena because in its context it makes specific reference to the plan and wisdom of God as manifested in the clouds and other weather phenomena. Verse 36 parts *a* and *b* are parallel and should be considered together. Verse 36 might be rendered: Who hath put wisdom in the cloud layers? Or who hath given understanding to the cloud formations?

The thought continues along the same lines in verse 37: "Who can number the clouds in wisdom?" (This probably refers to cloud formation and coverage rather than an actual physical count, as mentioned before.) "Who can stay the bottles of heaven?" The Hebrew word for *stay* is *shakah.* It literally means "to cause to lie down." Bottles are used for storage. This same idea of storage is expressed here; water is stored in a cloud as minute droplets, far too small to drop out of a cloud. If the cloud is full of moisture, the droplets increase in diameter until they are large enough to fall down. This conveys the idea that the droplets are pushed down or made to lie down. "If the clouds be full of rain, they empty themselves upon the earth" (Ecclesiastes 11:3).

All these phenomena are manifestations of God's divine wisdom, displayed by the intricate designs in nature.

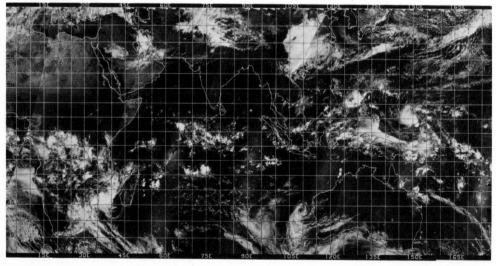

Photograph courtesy of National Weather Service, National Oceanic and Atmospheric Administration, Rockville, Md.

The spreading of the clouds

# 28

# The Spreading of the Clouds

Weather satellites can view one-half of the world at a glance and send back pictures. This data includes such information as high-low pressure areas, temperature, and cyclones. The data is sorted by a computer and printed on a map with a grid. The amount and type of cloud coverage can be transmitted within minutes as the clouds spread over the United States. Since infrared photography can continue weather surveillance during the night, a twenty-four hour watch can be maintained.

Tiros and ESSA weather satellites frequently show the frontal patterns and cloud formations over the United States and various parts of the world as the clouds spread from west to east. The spreading of the clouds is mentioned in Job 36:29, "Can any understand the spreading of the clouds?"

Below is a computer report of cloud coverage. The next time you watch the weather forecast and see the clouds spreading from west to east over the United States, remember the scientific question asked of Job.

## Cloud formation

"He causeth the vapours to ascend from the ends of the earth; he maketh lightnings for the rain; he bringeth the wind out of his treasuries" (Psalm 135:7).

# 29

# Cloud Formation

When vapors ascend from the earth, they cool and condense to form a cloud. Cloud formation over the ocean is indicated in Job 38:9. Clouds consist of minute water droplets or ice crystals which are smaller than rain drops. These minute cloud droplets are too small to fall out of a cloud; they must overcome the updrafts of warm air. Lightning may cause the formation of minute amounts of oxides of nitrogen that are extremely hygroscopic. These oxides of nitrogen along with numerous other particles of dust, smoke, salts, and sulfur dioxide constitute the highest part of the dust of the world. Scientifically, this dust is known as condensation nuclei. Minute cloud droplets gather on these nuclei to form droplets of rain large enough to fall out of a cloud.

Condensation nuclei are mentioned in Proverbs as the highest part of the dust of the world. Proverbs 8:22-36 illustrate the eternal nature of Wisdom, which we, from the New Testament perspective, equate with the Messiah. He existed before the highest part of the dust of the world was formed (before condensation nuclei were formed). This is a remarkable scientific statement. Our concept of condensation nuclei is a twentieth century idea about which very little is understood. And God said, "I was set up from everlasting, from the beginning, or ever the earth was. When there were no depths, I was brought forth; when there were no fountains abounding with water. Before the mountains were settled, before the hills was I brought forth. While as yet he had not made the earth, nor the fields, nor the highest part of the dust of the world. . . . For whoso findeth me findeth life, and shall obtain favor of the Lord" (Proverbs 8:23-35).

# 30

# The Numbering of the Clouds

Job was asked if he could number the clouds (Job 38:37). The Hebrew word for "number" can mean "tally," "score," "record," "recount," "cipher," or "count." In this reference the word may mean "record" or "take into consideration" the cloud coverage. The thought is not necessarily an individual count of each cloud, but a recording of cloud coverage. This is not to imply that God cannot count each cloud, for even the hairs of our heads are numbered (Matthew 10:30).

For example, the numbering of the clouds could refer to the total number of storm clouds covering the earth. There is a constant number of approximately 4,000 rainstorms striking the earth every twenty-four hours, and the number remains constant. Some observers count all atmospheric disturbances—not just rainstorms—and arrive at numbers as high as 10,000, but however storms are counted, the number remains constant. Storm clouds are necessary to mix the air between layers and remove pollution. Storms are also necessary to exchange charges of electricity between earth and atmosphere. Furthermore, nitrogen is returned to forests by lightning strokes. The consistency of the necessary rainstorms is evidence of the Creator. (For a discussion on the constant number of storm clouds on earth, see: U.S. Congress, Committee on Science and Technology, *Hearing on Atmosphere,* page 406, 1976).

The accompanying picture is a satellite photograph showing cloud coverage over the Holy Land. The Great Rift is clearly seen; the Sea of Galilee is to the left of the center. It is from the Mediterranean (far left) that the cyclonic storms lash the coastal area. This photograph is a reminder of the scientific question asked Job. Could Job number the clouds (or take into consideration the amount of cloud coverage)?

"Who can number the clouds in wisdom?" (Job 38:37).

Photograph courtesy of National Oceanic and Atmospheric Administration, Rockville, Md.

## Cloud coverage over Israel

This satellite photograph shows the amount of cloud coverage over Israel. In the photograph above, the white, puffy clouds over the Mediterranean region are fair-weather cumulus clouds. It is, however, from this area that the rain comes. This was noted by Jesus in the book of Luke. "And he [Jesus] said also to the people, When ye see a cloud rise out of the west, straightway ye say, There cometh a shower; and so it is" (Luke 12:54).

71

Photograph by Harold M. Lambert, Philadelphia, Pa.

## Lightning

"Who hath divided a watercourse for the overflowing of waters, or a way for the lightning of thunder; To cause it to rain on the earth, where no man is; on the wilderness, wherein there is no man" (Job 38:25-26).

Photograph by Harold M. Lambert, Philadelphia, Pa.

## Cloud balancing

Clouds are balanced in the air by two major forces. Gravity pushes down, warm air rises.

"Dost thou know the balancings of the clouds, the wondrous works of him which is perfect in knowledge?" (Job 37:16).

73

# 31

# Cloud Balancing

Heat from the sun is like a giant mixer that stirs up earth's atmosphere. When the sun's rays warm the earth, the air closest to the ground is also warmed. It is warmed unequally because of differences in soil, terrain, vegetation, and other factors. If the buoyancy of the rising air is sufficient, it carries water vapor and dust particles along with it. Surface air, including moisture and particles are accelerated upward and may consolidate into rising columns of air and eventually form a cloud. The downward pull of gravity on the droplets and particles is so small that they remain aloft. As the altitude increases, air pressure decreases and the rising moisture and particles encounter less resistance. Clouds are balanced by two major opposing forces, gravity and buoyancy due to updrafts of heated air.

In Job 37:16, Elihu acknowledged cloud balancing as one of the wondrous works of the Lord. The balance of the clouds is a modern scientific concept, yet it was mentioned in the Scripture thousands of years ago. All of these intricate designs in nature reveal the wondrous works of the Lord. The balance of the clouds is truly one of the wondrous works of the Lord. Through this delicate balance, the moisture and dust-laden clouds are kept aloft.

The weight of water vapor in a thick cloud may be a fantastic amount. Job 26:8 mentions the water bound up in a thick cloud, yet the cloud does not burst beneath the weight. In this verse the Old English word *rent* means "to tear into pieces." "He bindeth up the waters in his thick clouds; and the cloud is not rent under them." (Job 26:8).

When the minute droplets become large enough they will no longer float, but they rain down. "For he maketh small the drops of water: they pour down rain according to the vapour thereof" (Job 36:27).

# 32

# Lightning

Lightning is a result of the buildup of unlike charges within a storm cloud. The lightning stroke is a flow of electrical current. The charge in the clouds must be great enough to overcome the insulating effect of the air in order to conduct a flow of current. It heats the air and causes an explosive expansion, creating thunder. Lightning travels along a charged path several inches wide; the temperature of this path may be as much as 40,000°C. "The way [path] for the lightning of thunder," in Job 38:25, refers to this pathway.

Modern science recognizes two basic types of lightning—hot and cold. Cold lightning is a short stroke with very high current. Hot lightning has low current, lasts much longer, and usually burns whatever it strikes. The fact that hot lightning burns its target is suggested by loss of the flocks in Psalm 78. The Hebrew word translated *thunderbolt* literally means "burning heat." "He gave up their cattle also to the hail, and their flocks to hot thunderbolts" (Psalm 78:48).

Current experimental evidence indicates that whenever water vapor is sprayed into the area of an electrical discharge, drops are formed from the vapor. In a similar fashion, lightning provides the electrical charges necessary to make droplets unite. The relationship between lightning and rain is implied in Psalm 135:7b, "he maketh lightnings for the rain." Compare this with Job 38:25-26; Jeremiah 10:13, and 51:16. Controlling lightning and thunder is only part of the way God manifests His power. "Lo, these are parts of his ways: but how little a portion is heard of him? but the thunder of his power who can understand?" (Job 26:14).

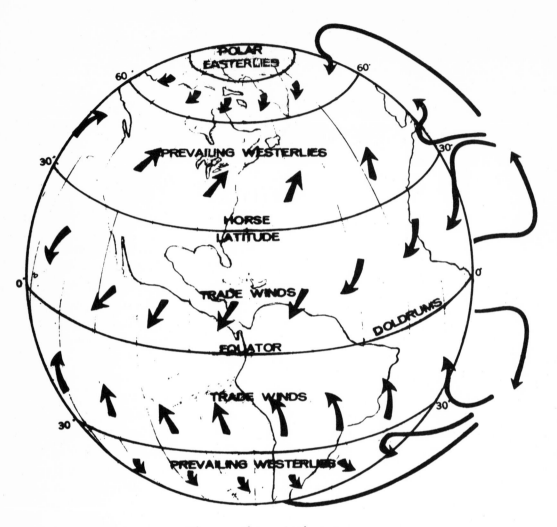

The earth's wind systems

Note the general pole-to-equator circulation, the whirling about (the Coriolis force), and the specific circuits.

"The wind goeth toward the south, and turneth about unto the north; it whirleth about continually, and the wind returneth again according to his circuits" (Ecclesiastes 1:6).

Those who apply this verse to local weather conditions in Palestine will have some difficulty. The air movement in the Mediterranean is generally north to south, but in summer it is deflected around a Cyprus low so that the resulting air masses generally move from west to east across Palestine. The winter rainy season is characterized by cyclonic storms which move in from the Mediterranean so that the general flow of air masses is from west to east.

76

# 33

# The Earth's Wind Systems

The wind systems of the earth are due primarily to two major influences: differences in the sun's radiation on various surfaces of the earth and earth's rotation. George Hadley, a seventeenth century scientist, was the first to propose a model on the pole-to-equator movement of air masses. He suggested that warm, moist air rises at the equator and moves toward the poles in a large, rotating pattern. Today this pattern is called a Hadley cell.

During the nineteenth century, G. G. Coriolis noticed that an object moving across a turning surface would veer off to the right or to the left, depending on the direction of rotation. William Ferrel (1856) recognized that this effect also applied to the rotation of the earth and the wind systems. This is known as Ferrel's law. This law states that winds in the northern hemisphere are deflected to the right and those in the southern hemisphere are deflected to the left. Earth's rotation causes the winds to veer off and pile up in some areas to form wind belts.

If the earth did not rotate, the cool air from the north pole would go to the equator, where it would be heated. Then the air would rise and return to the poles by the same pathway. The air would be cooled at the poles, contract, sink lower, and repeat its cycle. But the added effect of the rotation of the earth causes the winds to whirl about continually in the northern and southern hemispheres.

Thousands of years before these phenomena were discovered, the Scripture suggested them in Ecclesiastes 1:6. This verse suggests: (1) the general pole-to-equator circulation, (2) that the whirling about indicates the Coriolis force, and (3) that the wind has specific circuits.

# 34

# Air Pressure

The principle of the Torricelli barometer: pressure changes in the air change the height of the column of mercury. The Scripture says air has weight, or pressure. "To make the weight for the winds" (Job 28:25).

Pressure is the force that matter exerts on each unit of area it contacts, since air is gaseous matter, it also has weight and exerts pressure.

During the seventeenth century, Galileo observed that a suction pump would not raise water more than approximately thirty-four feet. He thought air had weight, but apparently he was not able to prove it. Evangelista Torricelli, a student of Galileo, suggested that if the air could support a column of water more than thirty feet high, then it could support a column of mercury about two and one-half feet since

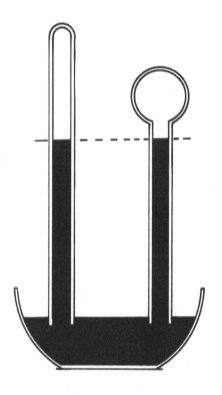

Torricelli barometer

mercury is roughly thirteen times as heavy as water. Torricelli was the first to make a barometer. He proved that air had pressure. Hundreds, and even thousands of years before Torricelli, the Scripture said air had weight.

# 35

# Frost

If the ground temperature drops below freezing during a clear night, ice particles are formed directly from water vapor in the air near the ground. This is called hoarfrost. Frost develops beautiful, feathery, crystal patterns on windowpanes as the primary frost begins to melt and then re-crystalizes. God's hand in nature is beautifully manifested in the crystal patterns of frost.

"He giveth snow like wool: he scattereth the hoarfrost like ashes" (Psalm 147:16).

Photograph by Harold M. Lambert, Philadelphia, Pa.

## Frost on a windowpane

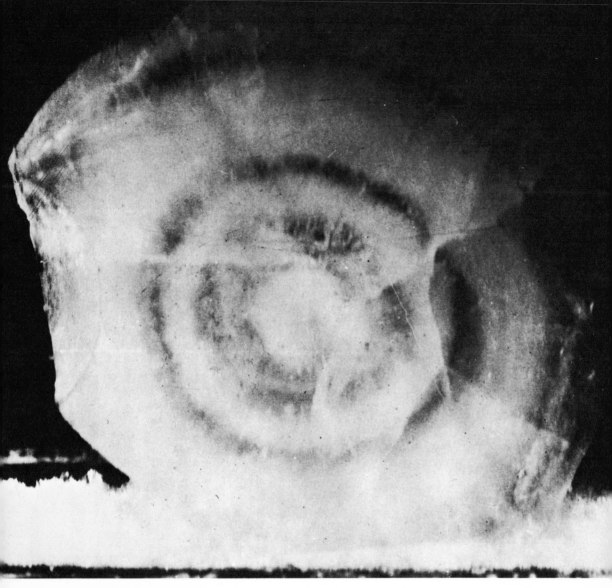

Photograph courtesy of National Weather Service, National Oceanic and Atmospheric Administration, Rockville, Md.

## Hail

Cross section through a hailstone showing the clear and opaque layers.

"And Moses stretched forth his rod toward heaven: and the LORD sent thunder and hail, and the fire ran along upon the ground; and the LORD rained hail upon the land of Egypt. So there was hail, and fire mingled with the hail, very grievous, such as there was none like it in all the land of Egypt since it became a nation. And the hail smote throughout all the land of Egypt all that was in the field, both man and beast; and the hail smote every herb of the field, and brake every tree of the field. Only in the land of Goshen, where the children of Israel were, was there no hail" (Exodus 9:23-26).

# 36

# Hail

Hail is formed in cumulonimbus clouds. Both ice crystals and water are present in this type of cloud, and both are probably required for hail formation. A cross section of a hailstone shows alternate layers of opaque and clear ice. These layers are primarily the result of ice pellets that pick up water in the supercool middle and upper regions of the storm cloud. The opaque and clear layers result from differences in the freezing rate and the rate at which the pellets accumulate water.

Hail is fairly common in the midwinter along the coastal plain of Palestine. The Bible mentions hail and hailstones several times in reference to divine judgment. The most notable of these was Joshua 10:11 in the Valley of Aijalon. Hail is also recorded as one of the plagues in Exodus 9:23-26. God used this natural phenomenon; the timing and the amount were miraculous. "He destroyed their vines with hail, and their sycamore trees with frost. He gave their cattle also to the hail, and their flocks to hot thunderbolts" (Psalm 78:47-48).

Hail is also mentioned in the book of Revelation as God's judgment during the Tribulation. The size of the hailstones that will fall will be a scientific wonder. The weight is said to be a talent—approximately 100 pounds.

"And there fell upon men a great hail out of heaven, every stone about the weight of a talent: and men blasphemed God because of the plague of the hail; for the plague thereof was exceeding great" (Revelation 16:21).

# 37

# Glaciation

Snow-capped Mount Ararat has a glacier that covers twenty-two square miles. There are twelve glacial fingers extending from the main cap. The elevation is 16,984 feet; glaciation starts at about 13,000 feet. Morris and Whitcomb, in *The Genesis Flood,* suggest that glaciation is the result of the flood. Rapidly frozen mammals seem to support this view, particularly where they are frozen with fresh food in their mouth.

God makes it clear that He is in control of all weather phenomena, even glaciers. "Out of whose womb came the ice? And the hoary frost of heaven, who hath gendered it?

The waters are hid as with a stone, and the face of the deep is frozen" (Job 38:29-30).

Photograph courtesy of John Morris, San Diego, Calif.

## Mount Ararat

# III

# CHEMISTRY

Photograph courtesy of Carolina Biological Supply Co., Burlington, N.C.

## The opium poppy

"They have him vinegar to drink mingled with gall [opium]: and when he had tasted thereof, he would not drink" (Matthew 27:34).

The opium poppy is used in the manufacture of several drugs such as codine, morphine, and narcotine. Opium was used by the Egyptians in ancient times.

# 38

# In an Atom of Time

An atom is the smallest particle that retains the characteristics of an element. Thus, it is indivisible: If the atom is divided it loses its elemental characteristics. The word *atom* is derived from a Greek word that means "uncut," or "indivisible." The Greek word *en atomo* occurs in 1 Corinthians 15:51-52, describing the smallest unit of time, "Behold I show you a mystery; we shall not all sleep, but we shall be changed, in a moment [*en atomo*], in the twinkling of an *eye*, at the last trump; for the trumpet shall sound, and the dead shall be raised incorruptible, and we shall be changed."

The Greek word for *atom* is *atomos,* which is derived from the base word *tomos,* which means "to cut." The *a* at the beginning (alpha privative), negates the word, making it *atomos,* which means "uncut," or "indivisible". In the Corinthian text, *en atomo* is in the locative case; the case of position or sphere. So the word might be translated, "the sphere of an atom." Thus, it is saying that we are to be changed within the realm of time of an atom.

In order to measure the rate of radioactive decomposition in bits of matter within the nucleus of an atom, it is necessary to divide a second into smaller units of time. The units given in the accompanying table are used in this kind of study.

## Table of Time

a micro second equals $1 \times 10^{-6}$ seconds or one millionth of a second

a nano second equals $1 \times 10^{-9}$ seconds or one billionth of a second

a pico second equals $1 \times 10^{-12}$ seconds or one trillionth of a second

The Greek word *en atomo* conveys the idea of the smallest possible fraction of time (that which is indivisible). At present, the smallest unit of time that can be measured is approximately $1 \times 10^{-16}$ seconds. In theory, measurement extends down to $1 \times 10^{-24}$ seconds, or perhaps even lower. For an illustration, let us use the pico second. Then it could be concluded that in one trillionth of a second we are to be changed. The apostle Paul did not want us to be ignorant of this fact.

> But I would not have you to be ignorant, brethren, concerning them which are asleep, that ye sorrow not, even as others which have no hope. For if we believe that Jesus died and rose again, even so them also which sleep in Jesus will God bring with him. For this we say unto you by the word of the Lord, that we which are alive and remain unto the coming of the Lord shall not prevent [precede] them which are asleep. For the Lord himself shall descend from heaven with a shout, with the voice of the archangel, and with the trump of God: and the dead in Christ shall rise first: then we which are alive and remain shall be caught up together with them in the clouds, to meet the Lord in the air: and so shall we ever be with the Lord. Wherefore comfort one another with these words (1 Thessalonians 4:13-18).

If the pico second illustrated above is the correct time element, then we could assume that all of the events of verses 16 and 17 must take place in one trillionth of a second.

# 39

# The Atoms Will Be Loosed

The universe is held together by three fundamental forces—nuclear force, electromagnetic force, and gravitational force. The most powerful of these is the nuclear force, which binds protons and neutrons together in the atomic nucleus. The nuclear force binds the particles of the nucleus into such a compact mass that the density exceeds a billion tons per cubic inch.

Second Peter 3:10-12 indicates these nuclear forces are to be loosed some day.

> But the day of the Lord will come as a thief in the night; in the which the heavens shall pass away with a great noise, and the elements shall melt with fervent heat, the earth also and the works that are therein shall be burned up. Seeing then that all these things shall be dissolved, what manner of persons ought ye to be in all holy conversation and godliness, looking for and hasting unto the coming of the day of God, wherein the heavens being on fire shall be dissolved, and the elements shall melt with fervent heat?

The word rendered "melt" in verses 10 and 12 is the Greek verb *luo*, "to loose." This indicates that the nuclear forces shall be loosed as seen in the words derived from the Greek verb luo: *luthesetai*—translated "melt" in verses 10 and 12; *luomenon*—translated "dissolved" in verses 11 and 12.

The word rendered "melt" in verses 10 and 12 is the Greek verb *luo*, to loose. This indicates that the nuclear forces shall be loosed as seen in the words derived from the Greek verb luo: *Luthesetai*—translated "melt" in verses 10 and 12; *luomenon*—translated "dissolved" in verses 11 and 12.

The word *luo* means "to loose something that is bound." It is used in a similar manner in Revelation 1:5 where it speaks of being loosed from our sins. "And from Jesus Christ, who is the faithful witness, the first-born of the dead, and the ruler of the kings of the earth. Unto him that loveth us, and loosed us from our sins by his blood" (ASV).

The Greek word *paraleusontai* translated "pass away" in verse 10 refers to what will happen; *luthesetai* and *luomenon* (will be loosed), tell how it will happen.

From the Greek text, it might be concluded that the chemical elements will literally be burned up because of the letting go of the nuclear forces that bind the protons and neutrons together in the atomic nucleus. This seems reasonable, since the Bible indicates that the Lord holds all things together. On the day of the Lord, all nuclear binding forces are set free. At present, the Lord is still the Sustainer of the universe and upholds all things by the Word of His power. He holds the atoms together and the universe in place; He is the sustaining power: "And he [Christ] is before all things, and by him all things consist [are held together]" (Colossians 1:17). "Upholding all things by the word of his power" (Hebrews 1:3*b*).

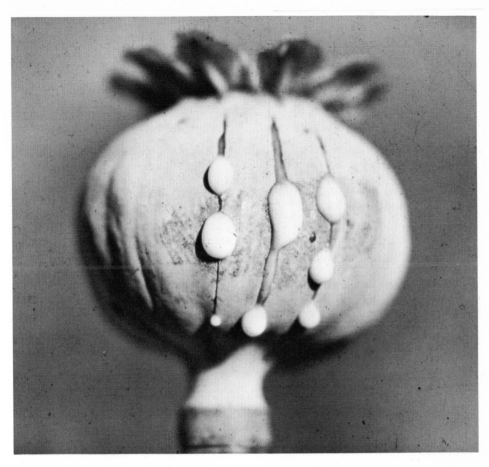

Photograph courtesy of Carolina Biological Supply Co., Burlington, N.C.

## Gall, or opium

Photograph of the opium poppy head which has been incised according to the oriental method for extracting the narcotic substance.

Psalm 69:21 was a prophecy concerning the Messiah. He was to be given gall and vinegar. This prophecy was fulfilled in Matthew 27:34 when Jesus was given the narcotic drink with vinegar. Note that after He tasted the drink, He refused it.

"They gave me also gall for my meat; and in my thirst they gave me vinegar to drink" (Psalm 69:21).

"They gave him vinegar to drink mingled with gall [opium]: and when he had tasted thereof, he would not drink" (Matthew 27:34).

89

# 40

# Gall—the Opium Narcotic Offered to Jesus

Jesus was offered gall and vinegar when He was on the cross (Matthew 27:34). Gall is the narcotic substance obtained from the opium poppy. The prophecy for this was in Psalm 69:21. The Hebrew word *rosh* is comparable to the word *head,* used to denote the conspicuous head of the opium poppy. *Gesenius Hebrew Dictionary* states that *rosh* refers to the opium poppy. This is consistant with the early works of Celsus (*De medicina,* 42 BC-AD 37), who considered gall a plant and not bile.

Opium is a latex exudated from the green buds of the opium poppy, *Papaver somniferum.* The exudate consists of a crude mixture containing at least twenty-five or more strong alkaloids. The buds are incised in two or three places; this is the oriental method of obtaining the exudate. Some of these alkaloids are very potent narcotics. The most important one is morphine. Morphine constitutes about 10 percent of the crude extract. Codine, a methyl ether of morphine, is present in approximately 3 percent. Papaverine is present in about 3 to 4 percent, and narcotine is present in lesser amounts. Different varieties of the poppy contain slightly different potencies of the narcotics.

There is disagreement about the effects of myrrh. Some consider it strongly analgesic; still others consider it to have only a mild soothing effect. A. T. Robertson suggests the myrrh may have been given in order to add a better flavor to the sour wine since the gall would have a bitter taste. Robertson further suggests that both substances may have been in the drink that Jesus refused. Jesus did not drink man's cup; He drank God's cup. "Then said Jesus unto Peter, Put up thy sword into the sheath: the cup which my Father hath given me, shall I not drink it?" (John 18:11).

# 41

# Drugs

The use of drugs has gained momentum during these last days of the church age. It will continue to do so and will be manifested during the Tribulation. There are some Greek words that indicate the use of drugs. The word translated *sorceries* in Revelation 9:21 and 18:23 is the Greek word *pharmakeia,* from which we derive our words pharmacy and pharmacist. The verses refer to the preparation or use of drugs.

A similar word, *pharmakeus,* is found in Revelation 21:8. The word refers to a person who prepares or administers drugs. The term could be applied to a dope pusher or a dope addict. *Pharmakeus* is translated "sorcerer" in the King James Version.

Galatians 5:20 uses the word *pharmakeia,* not in terms of the Tribulation, but with reference to the works of the flesh. *Pharmakeia* is translated *witchcraft* in this passage. "Now the works of the flesh are manifest, which are these; adultry, fornication, uncleanness, lasciviousness,

idolatry, witchcraft, hatred, variance, emulations, wrath, strife, seditions, heresies. Envyings, murders, drunkenness, revellings, and such like: of the which I tell you before, as I have also told you in time past, that they which do such things shall not inherit the Kingdom of God" (Galatians 5:19-21).

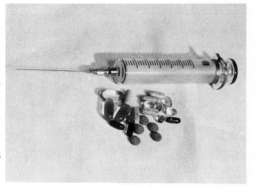

Photograph by Wolfe Worldwide Films, Los Angeles, Calif.

## An ancient winepress at Subeita

To make wine, fruit was trampled in a vat above, the juice ran down to the lower vat.

"Who hath woe? who hath sorrow? who hath contentions? who hath babbling? who hath wounds without cause? who hath redness of eyes? They that tarry long at the wine; they that go to seek mixed drink. Look not thou upon the wine when it is red, when it giveth his colour in the cup, when itmoveth itself aright. At the last it biteth like a serpent, and stingeth like an adder. Thine eyes shall behold strange women, and thine heart shall utter perverse things. Yea, thou shalt be as he that lieth down in themidst of the sea, or as he that lieth upon the top of a mast. They have stricken me, shalt thou say, and I was not sick; they have beaten me, and I felt it not: when shall I awake? I will seek it yet again" (Proverbs 23:29-35).

# 42

# Wine and Vinegar

Yeasts ferment sugar to form alcohol and carbon dioxide gas. If the fermenting process is maintained in the absence of atmospheric oxygen (anaerobic conditions), the resulting material will be wine, but if the fermenting liquid is exposed to air (aerobic conditions), the reaction goes on to form vinegar. Alcohol is actually an intermediate product. The alcoholic content of wine is around 12 to 13 percent when the reaction stops. The chemical reaction from fresh juice to wine is summarized in the first reaction below; the second step from wine to vinegar is also shown. This is a generalized chemical reaction; the process is far more complicated than this.

$$C_6H_{12}O_6 \quad\quad + \text{yeast} \quad\quad \longrightarrow \quad 2CH_3CH_2OH \quad + 2CO_2$$

Sugar from juice (enzymes) ethyl alcohol carbon dioxide

Anaerobic conditions

---

$$2CH_3CH_2OH \quad + 2O_2 \longrightarrow \quad 2CH_3COOH \quad + 2H_2O$$

Alcoholic liquid Acetobacter bacteria Acetic acid water

Aerobic conditions (vinegar)

---

The fruit of the vine has always been one of the most important crops of the Holy Land. Grapes are harvested around August or September, depending on the variety. The ancient winepress generally consisted of two vats, an upper and a lower one. The vats were hewn out of rock, or made by digging a hole into the earth and lining it with stones (Matthew 21:33). The lower vat (Greek *hupolenion*) caught the juice from the press. The fruit was pressed by treading with the bare feet and shouting (Isaiah 16:10).

93

The new wine, fresh juice before fermenting, was stored in vessels made from goat skins. If the fresh juice were put in used skins, the presence of fermentive organisms would cause the juice to ferment at once. The skins would burst because of the formation of carbon dioxide gas. "Neither do men put new wine into old wine-skins: else the skins burst, and the wine is spilled, and the skins perish: but they put new wine into fresh wine-skins, and both are preserved" (Matthew 9:17, ASV).

Instructions concerning fermentation products are given in Proverbs 23:31. Fresh grape juice is purple. As it ferments, the purplish color becomes reddish. "Don't look upon the wine when it is red," refers to the red, fermented wine. "When it moveth itself aright," refers to the movement brought about by the formation of bubbles of carbon dioxide during fermentation.

If wine is allowed to remain exposed to air in vats, a surface film forms on it. This film is composed of several microorganisms that chemically convert the wine to vinegar. One of the chief organisms found in this film is a bacterium called *acetobacter*. It was named because of its ability to oxidize alcohol to acetic acid (vinegar). Commercial vinegar contains approximately 4 percent acetic acid along with traces of esters, sugars, glycerin, and other substances that contribute to the flavor. If grapes or berries are used, the final product is sour wine, or wine vinegar. If apples are used, the final product is cider vinegar. Both are vinegar, but the names help identify the original source of the vinegar.

The Hebrew term *homez yayin* refers to wine vinegar. The wine in Mark 15:23 may refer to wine vinegar, or the Roman *acetum*. The general Hebrew term used to designate vinegar is *chometz* as in Psalm 69:21. In this psalm Messiah was to be given vinegar and gall (opium). The prophecy is shown fulfilled in the following references:

Vinegar mixed with gall (Matthew 27:34);
Sour wine, most likely wine vinegar, or Roman acetum, (Mark 15:23);
Vinegar, no mention of other ingredients, (Luke 23:36);
Vinegar, no mention of other ingredients, (John 19:29).

In Matthew 27:34, Jesus refused to drink the vinegar and opium mixture. The vinegar was given to the King of the Jews in mockery and so that the Scripture might be fulfilled. In traditional writings, the wicked are likened to vinegar; the good man who turns to wickedness is compared to sour wine—the same as wine turned to vinegar. Jesus did not turn to wickedness or sin—He was made sin, "For he hath made him to be sin for us, who knew no sin; that we might be made the righteousness of God in him" (2 Corinthians 5:21).

In the fermenting process, the fresh juice turns to wine and the wine turns to vinegar, provided certain conditions are present. The Hebrews used any stage of this as a drink, but alcohol was strictly forbidden in the tabernacle: "And the LORD spake unto Aaron, saying, Do not drink wine nor strong drink, thou, nor thy sons with thee, when ye go into the tabernacle of the congregation, lest ye die: it shall be a statute for ever throughout your generations" (Leviticus 10:8-9).

The word *wine* is frequently a translation of the Hebrew word *yayin,* or the Greek *oinos.* Both *yayin* and *oinos* may be used to describe fresh fruit or any stage of the fermentation process from juice to vinegar. For example, the Hebrew *yayin-mi-gat* refers to wine of the vat, which is freshly pressed juice. "And the threshing floors will be full of grain, and the vats will overflow with the new wine and oil" (Joel 2:24, New American Standard Bible).

In poetic terminology it is acceptable to gather wine instead of grapes. The word *wine* may also be substituted for the word *vine.* Also, in poetic language, wine usually occurs second in the triplet of corn, wine, and oil. In this triplet, the fresh fruit is intended, as in Deuteronomy 11:14: "I will give you the rain of your land in his due season, the first rain and the latter rain, that thou mayest gather in thy corn, and thy wine, and thine oil."

Grapes, rather than fermented wine, are signified by the use of the term *new wine* in Isaiah 65:8: "As the new wine is found in the cluster, and one saith, Destroy it not; for a blessing is in it."

From these references, it is concluded that *yayin* may refer to the fermented or the nonfermented drink, or fresh fruit. Note the following example: "and wine (*yayin*) that maketh glad the heart of man" (Psalm 104:15). In this verse, *yayin* possibly refers to the nonfermented drink because wine (*yayin*) or alcohol takes away the heart (Hosea 4:11).

The words *new wine* in both the Old and New Testaments may be used for either fermented or nonfermented drinks. The word *new* may refer to this year's vintage, but it may be fermented. In some cases, new wine may refer to the first drippings from the vat. See Hosea 4:11 and Acts 2:13 for the use of the term *new wine.* From these references, it must be concluded that *new wine* may refer to either fresh juice or an intoxicating drink.

In some cases, the context makes it clear whether the term is used to signify fresh or fermented juice, but in other places it is difficult to tell. Nevertheless, the Scripture is clearly against the use of intoxicating drinks. With such explicit instructions, it is difficult to conceive of Christ's making fermented wine. We are told to abstain from all appearance of evil (1 Thessalonians 5:22): we are not to be among winebibbers (Proverbs 23:20; and it is sin to offer a neighbor an intoxicating drink (Habbakuk 2:15).

Alcohol was used for medical purposes in ancient times. Up through the United States Civil War, alcohol was used as an anesthetic during operations. Wine was used in the Old and New Testament times for health reasons: "And the wine, that such as be faint in the wilderness may drink" (2 Samuel 16:2): "Drink no longer water, but use a little wine for thy stomach's sake and thine often infirmities" (1 Timothy 5:23).

A verse that is often improperly used to support the validity of drinking intoxicating beverages in moderation is Ephesians 5:18: "And be not drunk with wine, wherein is excess; but be filled with the Spirit." Paul is warning the Ephesian Christians to avoid anything that will lead them away from godly living.

The Bible gives numerous instructions concerning the drinking of alcoholic beverages:

Drinking alcoholic beverages becomes habitual:

"I will seek it yet again" (Proverbs 23:35b).

Drinking leads to poverty:

"For the drunkard and the glutton shall come to poverty" (Proverbs 23:21).

Alcohol affects the brain and causes vomiting:

"As a drunken man staggereth in his vomit" (Isaiah 19:14b).

Alcohol hinders moral judgment:

"But they also have erred through wine, and through strong drink are out of the way; . . . they err in vision, they stumble in judgment" (Isaiah 28:7).

Alcohol is deceiving:

"Wine is a mocker, strong drink is raging: and whosoever is deceived thereby is not wise" (Proverbs 20:1).

Drinking alcohol is associated with halucinations of adultery:

"Thine eyes shall behold strange women" (Proverbs 23:33a).

Drinking leads to perverse acts:

"And Noah awoke from his wine, and knew what his younger son had done unto him" (Genesis 9:24).

Drinking causes the utterance of perverse things:

"And thine heart shall utter perverse things" (Proverbs 23:33b).

Drinking leads to lawlessness:

"Lest they drink, and forget the law" (Proverbs 31:5).

Drinking leads away from heaven:

"Envyings, murders, drunkenness, revellings, and such like: of the which I tell you before, as I have also told you in time past, that they which do such things shall not inherit the kingdom of God" (Galatians 5:21).

The Bible gives definite instructions for the Christian. These instructions are repeated in various references but may be illustrated in Romans 13:13-14; "Let us walk honestly, as in the day; not in rioting and drunkenness, not in chambering and wantonness, not in strife and envying. But put ye on the Lord Jesus Christ, and make not provision for the flesh, to fulfill the lusts thereof."

# 43

# Leaven and the Fermentation Process

The word *leaven* comes from the Hebrew word *chamets,* which means "fermented." Since yeast cakes were not available in Old and New Testament times, a little ball of fermenting dough was used to make bread rise. Some of the dough was kept from one batch to the next to serve as a source of ferment. Thus, we have the comparison a little leaven leavens the whole lump (1 Corinthians 5:6).

Yeasts are fungi reproduced by budding; a bud is a small outgrowth of the cell. When yeast, sugar, and warm water are blended together, the yeast reproduces. The cells form rapidly, and soon the entire bowl is filled. This mixture is added to flour. Yeast cells ferment sugar with a subsequent release of carbon dioxide; the bubbles of carbon dioxide make the dough rise.

In Scripture leaven symbolizes sin. The very nature of leaven indicates that it represents evil; it causes the fermenting process. Yeast cells grow rapidly and make the dough puff up. When sin (leaven) enters, it spreads rapidly and causes the individual to become puffed up.

The symbolism of leaven and unleavened bread is best understood in several of the feasts of Israel. The first feast was the feast of the Passover (Leviticus 23:5). Christ represents the passover lamb, "For even Christ our passover is sacrificed for us" (1 Corinthians 5:7b). "When I see the blood, I will pass over you" (Exodus 12:13b). "The next day John seeth Jesus coming unto him, and saith, Behold the Lamb of God, which taketh away the sin of the world!" (John 1:29).

The second feast that illustrated the symbolism of leaven was the Feast of Unleavened Bread. This feast came the day after Passover. Note that unleavened bread represented the body of Christ.

"Seven days shall ye eat unleavened bread" (Exodus 12:15).

"And as they were eating, Jesus took bread, and blessed it, and brake it, and gave it to the disciples, and said, Take, eat; this is my body" (Matthew 26:26).

[Jesus said] "I am the living bread which came down from heaven; if any man eat of this bread, he shall live for ever; and the bread that I will give is my flesh, which I will give for the life of the world" (John 6:51).

The fourth feast was the Feast of Pentecost, also called the Feast of Weeks. This feast occurred fifty days after the Feast of Firstfruits. The remarkable thing about the Feast of Pentecost was the fact that it was observed with two loaves of bread baked with leaven. We can look back and see that the two loaves of bread baked with leaven represented Jew and Gentile, who are sinners and who make up the Body of Christ, His Church (Acts 2:1-21).

"Ye shall bring out of your habitations two wave loaves of two tenth deals; they shall be of fine flour; they shall be baked with leaven; they are the firstfruits unto the Lord" (Leviticus 23:17).

The accompanying drawing shows yeast cells; the large cells bud rapidly and make new cells. As they ferment sugar, they give off carbon dioxide gas, which is represented by the tiny circles between the cells.

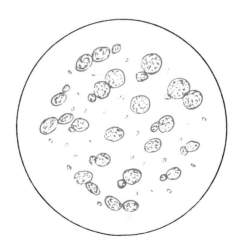

# 44

# Honey and the Fermentation Process

"No meat-offering, which ye shall bring unto the LORD, shall be made with leaven: for ye shall burn no leaven, nor any honey, in any offering of the LORD made by fire" (Leviticus 2:11).

Honey is a healthful food and is one of the purest foods known. Studies undertaken at the University of Maryland indicate that it has an inhibitory effect on the growth of microorganisms. Honey is a very tasty natural sweetner. "My son, eat thou honey, because it is good; and the honeycomb, which is sweet to thy taste" (Proverbs 24:13).

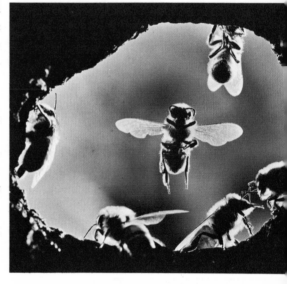

From the Moody Institute of Science film *City of the Bees*

Why was honey prohibited, along with leaven, from an offering? Leaven is indicative of fermentation, and it represents evil. Wine also represents the fermentation process, and it was forbidden to be drunk when in the tabernacle (Leviticus 10:8-9). In a similar manner, honey represents the fermentation process because it was used to make alcohol. In Bible times, honey was mixed with grain and fermented to make an alcoholic beverage.

Honey is used in Scripture in the comparative sense with reference to the judgments of the Lord. "The judgments of the LORD are true and righteous altogether. More to be desired are they than gold, yea, than much fine gold: sweeter also than honey and the honeycomb" (Psalm 19:9b-10).

DYE MUREX

Drawing by Alen Edgar, College Park, Md.

### Murex brandaris L

*Murex brandaris L* is the snail that provided the purple dye of ancient times. These snails are approximately 2½ to 3 inches long. Purple was used for royalty. "And Mordecai went out from the presence of the king in royal apparel of blue and white, and with a great crown of gold, and with a garment of fine linen and purple: and the city of Shushan rejoiced and was glad" (Esther 8:15). Concerning the kings of Midian, "And the weight of the golden earrings that he requested was a thousand and seven hundred shekels of gold; beside ornaments, and collars, and purple raiment that was on the kings of Midian, and beside the chains that were about their camels' necks" (Judges 8:26).

The gospel of Mark tells about the purple robe that was given to Jesus in mockery.

"And the soldiers led him away into the hall, called Praetorium; and they call together the whole band. And they clothed him with purple, and platted a crown of thorns, and put it about his head, and began to salute him, Hail, King of the Jews! And they smote him on the head with a reed, and did spit upon him, and bowing their knees worshipped him. And when they had mocked him, they took off the purple from him, and put his own clothes on him, and led him out to crucify him" (Mark 15:16-20).

# 45

# Purple Dye

The purple dye used in royal garments came from the murex snail. This snail was found along the Mediterranean coast. The scientific name of this snail was *Murex brandaris L.* The soft body parts of the snail provided only a drop of the material utilized as dye. This art of dyeing has been lost, and efforts to recapture it have failed. The only reference to where the purple dye came from is found in 1 Maccabees 4:23, where it is called "purple of the sea." In ancient times, the Phoenicians were very skillful in extracting and dyeing materials (Ezekiel 27:7, 16). Purple was used for the veil of the temple (2 Chronicles 2:14, 3:14). The Bible further states that Hiram was very skillful in dyeing and weaving the purple that King Solomon needed.

At a later date, the Greeks and Romans utilized the murex as a source of dye. Purple was a symbol of nobility and royalty. The Romans permitted senators and rulers to wear it, but others were forbidden to use it.

A careful study of the purple dye will clear up what seems to be a discrepancy in the Bible. In Mark 15:17 and John 19:2 it is stated that Jesus wore a purple robe, but in Matthew 27:28 the robe is called scarlet (*kokkinos*). The identification of colors is always subjective, but in this case the difference can be understood. Tyrian purple is purple with a reddish cast. Pliny called it a deep red-purple. The use of purple as a symbol of nobility and royalty may be illustrated by the garments of Mordecai (Esther 8:15). The purple robe that Jesus wore was in mockery. Christ, King of the Jews, did indeed wear a royal purple robe.

Drawing by Alen Edgar, College Park, Md.

## Coccus worm

The coccus worm, or scale insect, attaches itself to a tree and secretes the substance from which scarlet and crimson dyes are made. The following psalm shows the context in which the coccus worm is used to depict Christ on the cross (compare Matthew 27:46 and Mark 15:34).

"My God, my God, why hast thou forsaken me? Why art thou so far from helping me, and from the words of my roaring? O my God, I cry in the daytime, but thou hearest not; and in the night season, and am not silent. But thou are holy, O thou that inhabitest the praises of Israel. Our fathers trusted in thee: they trusted, and thou didst deliver them. They cried unto thee, and were delivered: they trusted in thee, and were not confounded. But I am a worm [coccus worm], and no man; a reproach of men, and despised of the people" (Psalm 22:1-6).

"Come now, and let us reason together, saith the LORD: though your sins be as scarlet (Hebrew *shanti*), they shall be as white as snow; though they be red like crimson (Hebrew *tola*), they shall be as wool" (Isaiah 1:18).

103

# 46

# Scarlet and Crimson Dyes

The scarlet and crimson dyes of the Bible were prepared by grinding the dried bodies of scale insects. The Egyptians used the dye as early as 3000 B.C. During the Middle Ages, landlords accepted the dye as payment for rent. The tenant must have worked hard in order to get enough for rent money, because it took about 70,000 insects to prepare one pound of dye.

In the Bible, the words *scarlet* and *crimson* are translated from various terms. The Hebrew words *tola* and *shani,* are used to denote a scarlet color made with dye from a worm, or insect larva. The Greek term for scarlet, *kokkinos,* is similar to the Latin *coccus,* from which comes the name for *Coccus ilicis,* a scale insect. Current textbooks use the term *Kermes ilicis* instead of *Coccus ilicis,* because this is the scale found on the *Kermes* oak in the Mediterranean area. This scale insect should be distinguished from the Mexican coccus worm, which is known as *Dactylopium coccus.* Both of these scale insects produce scarlet and crimson dyes. *Dactylopius* produces carminic acid; *Kermes* produces kermesic acid. These two substances are chemically related.

The scale insect attaches itself to a tree. Within the scale, it secretes a substance which makes the scarlet and crimson dye. This substance gives life to the young. This is the thought put forth in Psalm 22:6 which is prophetic of Christ's death on the cross. In this verse He is portrayed as a scarlet worm which gives his life. This prophetic picture is seen as complete in 1 Peter 2:24, where it speaks of Christ upon the tree, "Who his own self bare our sins in his body upon the tree."

Photograph courtesy of N. Z. Cherkis, Temple Hills, Md.

## The ocean, the source of rain

"He calleth for the waters of the sea, and poureth them out upon the face of the earth: The LORD is his name" (Amos 9:6).

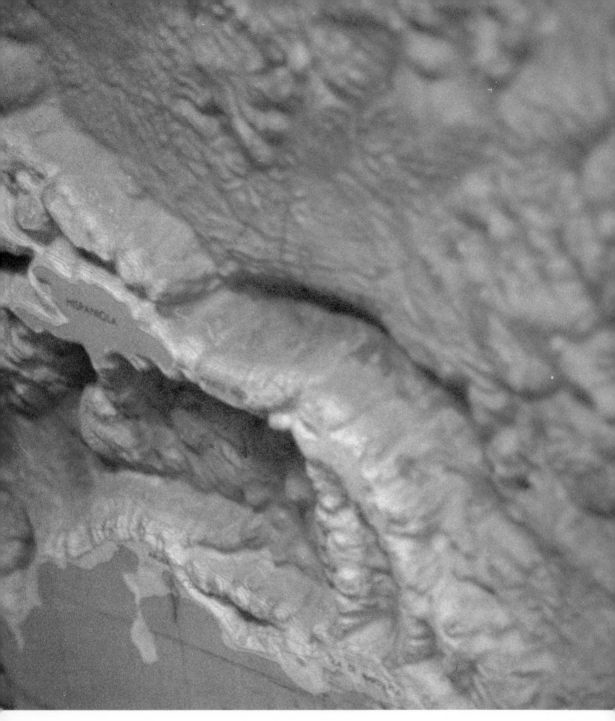

## The deep places

The Puerto Rico trench's greatest depth is known as the Milwaukee Depth. This photograph is of a model constructed from oceanographic charts.

"For I know that the LORD is great, and that our LORD is above all gods. Whatsoever the LORD pleased, that did he in heaven, and in earth, in the seas, and all deep places" (Psalm 135:5-6).

# IV

# OCEANOGRAPHY

# 47

# The Deep Places

A trench is a long, narrow depression in the ocean floor that looks like an enormous gash with very steep sides. The topography and depth of trenches distinguish them from all other valleys and depressions in the ocean floor. Trenches are found in the three major oceans, but the Pacific Ocean is unique because it has a semicontinuous peripheral belt of trenches and deep sea troughs. Extensive studies have been conducted on the Marianas Trench off the coast of Guam. The bathyscaph *Trieste* has traveled down almost seven miles into that trench. The best-known trench is perhaps the one off the coast of Puerto Rico; its deepest point is known as the Milwaukee Depth.

The Scripture makes reference to great oceanic depths by use of the Hebrew word *tehom,* (see ''great deep,'' Hebrew *tehom* in Genesis 7:11). Trenches have the greatest depths in the ocean floor, and the use of the Hebrew word seems to identify them. *Tehom* could be translated as ''abyssal depth.''

Land rifts, as well as marine rifts, occur in the earth's crust. One of the most notable land rifts is the Great Rift Valley, which extends from east Africa through the Holy Land. The Jordan valley is a part of this rift. The Hebrew word used for land depths is *mechgar.* In the following psalm, the psalmist mentions the deep places of the earth. Compare this with Psalm 135:6, which speaks of oceanic depths.

''For the LORD is a great God, and a great King above all gods, In his hand are the deep places of the earth: the strength of the hills is his also. The sea is his, and he made it; and his hands formed the dry land. O come, let us worship and bow down; let us kneel before the LORD our maker'' (Psalm 95:3-6).

# 48

# Mountains in the Sea

Until recently, the ocean floor was believed to be flat like the floor of a lake (reported in *Exploring the Ocean World* edited by Idyll). It is now known that seamounts are found throughout the oceans. As a general rule, seamounts are isolated peaks. Mountains underwater are not restricted to isolated seamounts; one of the largest mountain ridges on earth is the Mid-Oceanic Ridge, which zigzags about 35,000 miles. This ridge was discovered in 1873 by the H.M.S. *Challenger.* Detailed studies were first undertaken in 1925 by the German oceanographic research ship known as *The Meteor.* During World War II another type of mountain, the guyot, was discovered. Guyots are flat-topped seamounts.

It is interesting to note that prior to the ninteenth century, the idea of mountains in the sea was not scientifically accepted. God's Word said there were mountains in the sea. In the second chapter of Jonah, verses 3 through 6 are in retrospect. Jonah reviews his fall into the water and his being swallowed by a fish. The water compassed him about, and seaweed wrapped around his head (v. 5). He went down to the bottom of the mountains, the seamounts (v. 6). The earth with her bars refers to the rough or jagged edges. The mountains in Jonah 2:6 must be interpreted as seamounts, because Jonah said he was compassed about by the floods, seaweed (*suph*) wrapped around his head, and then he went down to the bottoms of the mountains.

Jonah left from the coast of Joppa, (Jonah 1:3), which is the modern city of Tel Aviv. Tarshish is believed by some to be the British Isles; others think it is the coast of Spain. Almost any route he had taken would have placed him in the area of seamounts.

# 49

# The Density of Water

Density is defined as the amount of matter per unit volume of a given substance: density = mass/volume. In terms of the metric system, density may be stated as the number of grams (mass) per cubic centimeter (volume). The density of water is 1.0 because 1 cubic centimeter of water weighs 1 gram (under specific temperature and pressure).

The density of water serves as a standard of comparison for specific gravity calculations in chemistry. Specific gravity is the comparison of the weight of a material or object with the weight of an equal volume of water. Ice has a density of $0.92$ g/cm$^3$. Thus, it is a little lighter than water and will float. This extremely important phenomenon preserves life in ponds and lakes.

The density of water is implied in Job 28:25b where it indicates weight or mass/volume relationship. This statement was made thousands of years before man acknowledged the density of materials in chemistry.

God's word says "He weigheth the waters by measure" (Job 28:25b).

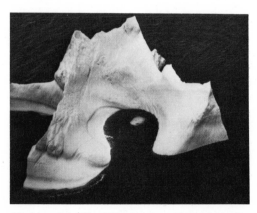

Photograph by Harold M. Lambert, Philadelphia, Pa.

### An iceberg

Ice floats because its density is $0.92$ g/cm$^3$ as compared to water which is $1.0$ g/cm$^3$. In this respect, water does not behave like other substances. This miracle of the Creator aids in keeping aquatic life from freezing.

111

"He layeth up the depth in storehouses"
(Psalm 33:7b).

## The ocean and oceanic reservoirs

The planet earth might well have been called the water planet. It is unique in the solar system because it has a temperature within the narrow range where water remains a liquid. The unusual properties of water—solid, gas, and liquid—were designed by the Creator to make the earth habitable. Although most of the earth is covered with water, God has placed certain limitations on it.

"Who shut up the sea with doors, when it brake forth, as if it had issued out of the womb? When I made the cloud the garment thereof, and thick darkness a swaddling band for it, and brake up for it my decreed place, and set bars and doors, and said, Hitherto shalt thou come, but no further: and here shall thy proud waves be stayed?" (Job 38:8-11).

# 50

# The Ocean and Oceanic Reservoirs

Approximately 71 percent of the earth's surface is covered with water. Science recognizes one communicating mass of water, which is sometimes called the "world ocean." The one ocean concept is indicated in Genesis 1:9: "And God said, Let the waters under the heaven be gathered together unto one place." It is customary to divide the water of the earth into four major divisions: the Atlantic, Pacific, Indian, and Arctic Oceans. It is significant that in Genesis 1:9 the waters are gathered together in one place, yet these are called "seas." The use of the plural for *seas* suggests the division into oceans.

If the surface of the globe were smooth, water would cover the earth 12,000 feet high (reported in *The Sea* by Leonard Engel and the editors of *Life*). The individual oceans have great recesses and trenches so that vast amounts of water can be stored at abyssal depths. Mt. Everest (29,028 ft.) could easily be sunk into the abyssal depths. An interesting scientific statement is found in Psalm 33. This statement indicates that there are oceanic storehouses for water. "He gathereth the waters of the sea together as an heap; he layeth up the depth in storehouses" (Psalm 33:7).

Job 38:8 makes reference to the limits or boundaries of the oceans, by use of the phrase "shut up the sea with doors." Job 38:9 describes the birth of the ocean and cloud formation. This oceanic baby was swaddled by a band of "thick darkness." This band of "thick darkness" was the band of clouds that surrounded the oceans. As water evaporates from the ocean, a band of clouds forms along the horizon. Job 38:10 is an allusion to the rocks and cliffs that form the shoreline. Job 38:11 implies that its waves can go just so far and no more. "When the waves thereof arise, thou stillest them" (Psalm 89:9*b*).

Photograph by V. T. Stringfield, U.S. Geological Survey, Denver, Colo.

## Springs of the sea

Pictured above is a submarine spring off the coast of Crescent Beach, Florida in St. Johns County. The spring forms the smooth surface in the background. In the following verse, the use of the Hebrew word *tehom* for depth implies the springs may be coming from the abyssal depths. "Hast thou entered into the springs of the sea? Or hast thou walked in the search of the depth?" (Job 38:16).

# 51

# Springs of the Sea

A spring is water which comes forth from the earth; a submarine spring is water which issues from the earth beneath the sea. The reference to springs of the sea in Job 38:16 means submarine springs. The record in Job is centuries before the first mention of submarine springs, although the Greeks and Romans did know about them at a very early date. The first nonbiblical reference to submarine springs appears to be around 63 B.C.—A.D. 21 when the Roman geographer, Strabo, recorded their occurrence.

Various places throughout the world have reported submarine springs. They are fairly common along the coast of Greece, Italy, Israel, and Syria. The South Sea Islands also have an abundance of fresh water springs. A large number of these originate in underwater volcanoes. Off the coast of Australia, fresh water may be dipped in abundance from the sea. The exact mechanism for the appearance of the fresh water is not clearly understood. On December 9, 1976 the *Washington Star* reported that the U.S. Geological Survey had discovered fresh water under the Atlantic. The fresh water extended beneath the continental shelf from Georges Bank off New England to the coast of Georgia. This merely confirms the truth of the Scripture.

Millions of gallons of fresh water are pouring into the salt water at vast rates. In recent years scientists have studied underwater springs because they provide millions of gallons of fresh water. This water is a potential storehouse of unpolluted water for large cities. An entire city could be supplied from such springs, but the cost would be enormous.

## Channels of the sea

Sea channels are valleys in the ocean floor. The type of valley shown in the photograph is a portion of a submarine canyon. It has high limestone walls. A deep-sea diver goes down to explore the canyon. Information regarding sea channels was recorded almost 3,000 years ago. "And the channels of the sea appeared" (2 Samuel 22:16).

# 52

# Channels of the Sea

Second Samuel 22 is a song of deliverance and thanksgiving by David. He makes frequent reference to natural occurrences, such as lightning, thunder, and winds. There is a tremendous scientific statement in verse 16 concerning the channels of the sea. Sea channels are a twentieth-century discovery, and it is amazing to find such an idea expressed here. A sea channel is a valley in the ocean floor. There are various types of valleys in the sea floor; they are named according to their shape or location. For example, there are deep-sea, interplain, and leveed channels. Deep-sea channels are usually part of a submarine canyon system which cuts through the continental shelf. These channels are quite large; some exceed Grand Canyon. Numerous tributary channels pass through the sea channels.

Most channels have been filled with sediment and can be recognized only by seismic profiling and drilling. One channel across the continental shelf off Hudson River is so large, however, that it is not yet filled. For information on topography and sedimentation of channels, see Menard, H. W., "Deepsea Channels, Topography, and Sedimentation" in *The Bulletin of the American Association of Petroleum Geologists,* volume 39, 1955.

How the submarine canyons and their associated system of sea channels were formed is a source of controversy. It was originally thought that sea channels were formed when glaciers melted and increased the water in the oceans. This theory has largely been abandoned. It seems more likely that shelf submarine canyons and their associated sea channels are drowned river valleys that formed during the flood. This explanation seems best because sea channels are located primarily where river valleys enter the coast or where a river previously entered the coast and recently has been diverted. This explanation would not apply to all valleys in the ocean floor. Some appear to be of an entirely different origin.

Photograph by USNS *Mizar,* courtesy of the Naval Research Laboratory, Washington, D.C.

## The paths of the sea—ocean currents

This deep-sea photograph from USNS *Mizar* was taken March 1973, in the northeast Atlantic. The path marks are caused by deep-sea currents. Worm tubes protrude and bend in the direction of the currents; these look like small palm trees.

"Thus saith the LORD, which maketh a way in the sea, and a path in the mighty waters" (Isaiah 43:16).

# 53

# The Paths of the Sea— Ocean Currents

In ancient times, very little was known or understood about ocean currents. During the fifteenth century, Prince Henry of Portugal recognized ocean currents and suggested they be studied. Another pioneer in observing ocean currents was Benjamin Franklin. When Franklin was postmaster general, he noticed that ships crossing the Atlantic were delayed as much as two weeks because of the currents. He studied the currents while on a ship and identified the Gulf stream current. He erroneously attributed it to the trade winds only.

Matthew Fontaine Maury in 1860 was the first to suggest that the ocean was a circulating system. He recognized this from reading Psalm 107:25. He was also the first to undertake a systematic collection of oceanographic data. His book on physical oceanography is still considered a basic text for studies of wind and current interaction (*Encyclopedia of Oceanography*, 1966, pg. 612).

Until the 20th century, the ocean bottom was considered devoid of currents. The work of G. Wust (1933, 1955, and 1957) showed fairly strong ocean bottom currents in the South Atlantic. His work was not supported by direct current measurements; therefore, his data was questioned by some oceanographers. With improved photographic techniques, his work has been proved correct.

The work of B. Heezen and C. Hollister (1964), with the aid of modern photographic techniques, showed ripple and scour marks in abyssal depths. The effect of currents on bottom sediments is seen by these ripples. As the currents pass over the bottom sediment, they leave a path of ripple marks. Any current in the sea may be rightfully called a path, but surely these literal paths on the bottom sediment give evidence of the truth of Psalm 8:8: "whatsoever passeth through the paths of the seas."

## The pathfinder of sea paths

The inscription on the Maury monument in Goshen, Virginia reads: "Matthew Fontaine Maury, pathfinder of the seas, the genius who first snatched from the ocean and atmosphere the secret of their laws. Born January 14, 1806. Died at Lexington, Virginia, February 1, 1873. Carried through Goshen Pass to his final resting place in Richmond, Virginia. Every mariner for countless ages, as he takes his chart to shape his course through the seas, will think of thee. His inspiration Holy Writ, Psalms 8 and 107, Verses 8, 23, and 24. Ecclesiastes Chapter 1 Verse 8. A Tribute by his Native State, Virginia, 1923." This photograph shows a statue of Maury located in Richmond, Virginia.

# 54

# The Paths of the Sea
# and the Pathfinder

Matthew Fontaine Maury (1806-1873) discovered the paths of the sea by reading about them in the Psalms; he is known as the pathfinder of the seas. The verses that inspired him were Psalm 8:8, Psalm 107:23-24, and Ecclesiastes 1:8 (Ecclesiastes 1:7 in the KJV). These verses describe the paths of the sea and the water cycle.

*Matthew Fontaine Maury, Pathfinder of the Seas,* written by Charles L. Lewis and published in 1927 by the U.S. Naval Institute, recounts many incidents in Maury's life. According to his life story, Maury was once confined to bed during an illness. Each night, his son read the Scripture to him. When the boy read Psalm 8:8, "The fish of the sea, and whatsoever passeth through the paths of the seas," he saw, in this passage, the paths of the sea. Maury said, "If God said there are paths in the sea, I am going to find them when I get out of this bed."

Maury reasoned there must be specific patterns of wind and water movement that created paths and would allow a ship to move faster in the water. He was the first to recognize that the ocean was a circulating system with interaction between wind and water. He made detailed studies of winds and currents from ship's logs. By taking advantage of these winds and currents, he plotted ship routes across the ocean. These routes form the basis of an international agreement. His work enabled shipping companies to save thousands of dollars and reduce the possibility of accidents.

Maury's native state of Virginia paid a tribute to him in 1923. Monuments of Maury were placed in Richmond and Goshen, Virginia. The inscription tells how Maury was inspired by reading the Bible.

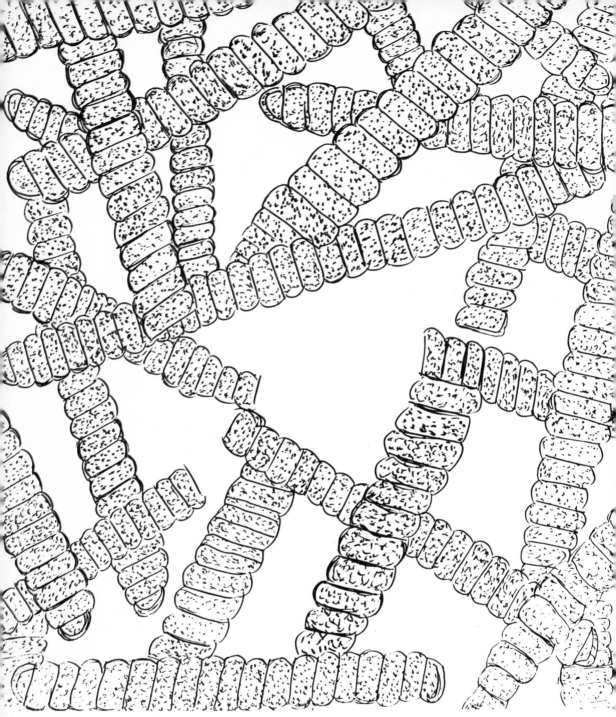

*Trichodesmium erythracum,* the algae of the Red Sea;
a drawing greatly enlarged

"O give thanks unto the LORD . . . To him which divided the Red Sea
into parts: for his mercy endureth for ever: and made Israel to pass
through the midst of it: for his mercy endureth for ever: but overthrew
Pharaoh and his host in the Red sea: for his mercy endureth for ever"
(Psalm 136:1a, 13-15).

# 55

# The Sea of Reeds or the Red Sea?

In modern times the Red Sea refers to the main part of the Gulf of the Indian Ocean that separates Egypt from Arabia. It extends from the Straits of Aden to the Sinai Peninsula. In ancient times the Red Sea included the Gulfs of Suez and Aqabah. The Hebrew name translated "Red Sea" in the King James Version is *Yam Suph,* which means "Sea of Reeds." Many Jewish scholars still call it the Sea of Reeds.

*Gesenius Hebrew and Chaldee Dictionary* renders *suph* as "rush," "reed," or "seaweed." From a botanical view, *rush* and *reed* are general terms that might be considered synonymous; thus, we are left with just two terms with which to deal: *reed* and *seaweed.* The word *seaweed* is the English equivalent of the Latin word *alga* (plural algae). In Exodus 2:3, the basket that held baby Moses was made of *suph* (reeds). Here the term *suph* must be rendered "reeds," because algae would not be used for such a basket. Jonah 2:5, says that *suph* (seaweed) wrapped around Jonah's head. The text seems to demand that *suph* be translated seaweed, or algae, because Jonah is out in the sea, not in the marshes. From these two references we may conclude that the Hebrew *suph* may be rendered either "reeds" or "seaweed."

The first appearance in which the word *red* designates the Red Sea is found in the Apocrypha. Several references are made in 1 Maccabees 4:9, Wisdom 10:18, and others. The Maccabees cover the period of history around 175-136 B.C. From this it may be concluded that the term has been in use for a long time. In the Septuagint, the term is given in the Greek *he eruthra thalassa;* a comparable term is found in early Latin writings as *mare rubrum* or *mare erythraeum.*

Numerous explanations have been given for the name *Red Sea.* The sea has red coral, red soil reflects its color in the sea, and red storks inhabit the areas around the sea. But it seems more likely that the term *red* is correlated with the original word *suph* (seaweed, or algae). Prior to the Maccabean era, the Hebrews called it the Sea of Reeds. No doubt this was the original meaning, and *reeds* most likely made reference to those along the Gulfs of Aden and Aqabah.

Current oceanographic studies of the Red Sea show 19 mg/m$^3$ for the chlorophyll productivity. This chlorophyll content indicates a rather low algal content. However, occasionally very high rates have been obtained. The alga *Trichodesmium erythraeum* sporadically increases in the Red Sea, giving a very high chlorophyll content. Such increases in algal content are referred to as algal bloom. The word *bloom* merely means an abundance of algae; algae are non-flowering plants. *Trichodesmium erythraeum* is a blue-green alga which has a red accessory pigment known as phycoerythrin. The refractibility of its pseudo-vacuoles gives the characteristic color. When the cells deteriorate, the red pigment leaks into the water, giving it a reddish cast.

No discussion of the Red Sea would be complete without mentioning the crossing of the Red Sea by the children of Israel. Various attempts have been made to explain away the miraculous nature the text seems to demand. "The flowing waters stood up like a heap; the deeps were congealed in the heart of the sea" (Exodus 15:8*b, c*, NASB). The use of the word *congealed* demands a miraculous interpretation. The wind would not hold the waters in a heap.

God's timing was perfect. He held the water up long enough to allow the Israelites to pass through the sea. As the Egyptians began to pass through the sea, the water fell back, drowning many soldiers.

In modern times, the Rabbi's Bible still uses the term, *Sea of Reeds.* This seems to be the original name of the Red Sea. The change of the name to the Red Sea appears to have taken place around the period of the Maccabees. The word *red* was most likely derived from the sporadic occurrence of the alga *Trichodesmium erythraeum.*

## The Song of Moses

"I will sing unto the Lord,
For He has triumphed gloriously;
The horse and his rider
He has hurled into the sea.
The Lord is my strength and song,
For He has brought me salvation.

This is my God, and I will glorify Him,
My father's God, whom I shall extol.
The Lord is a man of war,
The Lord is His name.
Pharaoh's chariots and his host
He has cast into the sea;
And his chosen captains
Are sunk in the *Sea of Reeds*.
The deeps cover them;
They went down into the depths like a stone.
Thy right hand, O Lord, is glorious in power,
Thy right hand, O Lord, shatters the enemy!
And in the greatness of Thy triumph
Thou overthrowest Thine adversaries.

Thou sendest forth Thy wrath,
And it consumes them like straw.
At the blast of Thy nostrils the waters were piled up,
The floods stood upright as a wall;
The deeps were congealed in the heart of the sea.
The enemy said:
'I will pursue, I will overtake,
I will divide the spoil;
My desire shall be satisfied upon them;
I will draw my sword,
And my hand shall destroy them.'
Thou didst blow with Thy wind, and the sea covered them;
They sank like lead in the mighty waters
Who is like Thee, O Lord, among the mighty?
Who is like Thee, glorious in holiness.
Awe-inspiring, doing wonders?
The Lord shall reign for ever and ever."

(Quoted from the Rabbi's Bible I,
by permission of Behrman House, Inc.
New York, New York, italics added.)

Photograph courtesy of National Aeronautics and Space Administration, Washington, D.C.

This view of Ethiopia and Somalia in northeast Africa shows the Red Sea and the Gulf of Aden.

The earth is the LORD'S, and the fulness thereof; the world, and they that dwell therein.

For he hath founded it upon the seas, and established it upon the floods (Psalm 24:1-2).

# V

# EARTH SCIENCE

## The midst of the earth

Mount Tabor rises out of the Plain of Esdraelon; Mount Tabor is not the only place that is called the navel of the earth. Mount Gerizim is also called the navel. "And Gaal spake again and said, See there come people down by the middle [Hebrew *tabur*—navel] of the land, and another company come along by the plain of Meonenim" (Judges 9:37). The Holy Land is considered the central point of the earth as shown by the fact that all other parts of the earth are referred to as the furtherest bounds. "The confidence [hope] of all the ends of the earth, and of them that are afar off upon the sea" (Psalm 65:5*b*).

# 56

# The Midst of the Earth

Traditionally, Jerusalem has been considered the center of the earth. By medieval tradition, the church of the Holy Sepulcher was considered the central point. The Greeks attempted to copy the idea for their false gods. According to Greek mythology, Delphi of ancient Greece was the center of the earth. The exact spot was marked by a stone known as the *Omphalos,* which means navel. According to mythology, two eagles starting from opposite ends of the earth met at this point. The fact that the Greeks used this idea for their false gods is strongly suggestive that the Holy Land was truly God's appointed center of the earth. The Scripture supports this view in various places by using the phrase "navel of the earth" and by indicating that all other places are at remote distances from it. "That dwell in the midst [navel] of the earth" (Ezekiel 38:12). "They also that dwell in the uttermost parts are afraid at thy tokens: thou makest the outgoings of the morning and evening to rejoice" (Psalm 65:8). "For God is my King of old, working salvation in the midst [navel] of the earth" (Psalm 74:12).

Andrew Wood, a physicist, has computerized the data on the earth's land masses in order to determine the approximate center of the surface of the earth. Wood's data indicates that the center of the earth is near Ankara, the present capital of Turkey, at 39° latitude and 34° longitude, on the same latitude as Mount Ararat and essentially the same longitude as Jerusalem. The data suggests the Holy Land was truly God's center of the earth. The Lord has promised that in the future Israel will be made the center of the nations politically and economically. The Lord said Israel would be the head, not the tail of the nations. "And the LORD shall make thee the head, and not the tail" (Dueteronomy 28:13a).

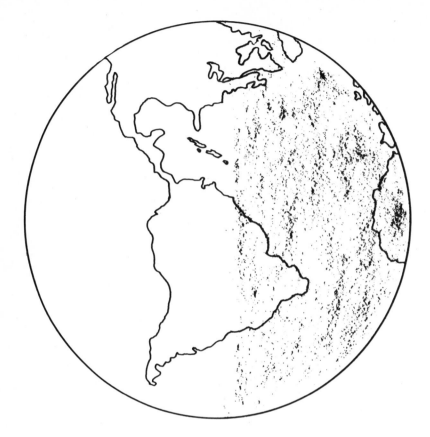

In that day————In that night

The earth is almost a perfect sphere. The polar diameter is approximately 26 miles shorter than the equatorial diameter.

"Have ye not known? have ye not heard? hath it not been told you from the beginning? have ye not understood from the foundations of the earth? It is he that sitteth upon the circle [sphere] of the earth, and the inhabitants thereof are as grasshoppers; that stretcheth out the heavens as a curtain, and spreadeth them out as a tent to dwell in" (Isaiah 40:21-22).

A round earth is implied in Luke where Jesus indicated that night and day occur simultaneously upon the earth.

"In that day, he which shall be upon the housetop, and his stuff in the house, let him not come down to take it away: and he that is in the field, let him likewise not return back. I tell you, in that night there shall be two men in one bed; the one shall be taken, and the other shall be left" (Luke 17:31,34).

130

# 57

# The Spherical Earth

The biblical cosmology in Job 26:7-10 suggests a round earth suspended in space. A literal translation of Job 26:10 is "He has described a circle upon the face of the waters, until the day and night come to an end." A spherical earth is also described in Isaiah 40:21-22. The Hebrew record is the oldest, because Job is one of the oldest books in the Bible. Historians generally credit the Greeks with being the first to suggest a spherical earth. In the sixth century B.C., Pythagoras suggested a spherical earth; in the third century B.C., Eratosthenes calculated the size of the earth. The Greeks also drew meridians and parallels. They identified such areas as the poles, equator, and tropics. This spherical earth concept did not prevail; the Romans drew the earth as a flat disk with oceans around it.

Proverbs 8:27 suggests a round earth by use of the word *circle* (NASB). If you are overlooking the ocean, the horizon appears as a circle. This circle on the horizon is described in Job 26:10 (NASB). The circle on the face of the waters is one of the proofs that the Greeks used for a spherical earth. Yet here it is recorded in Job, ages before the Greeks discovered it. Job 26:10 indicates that where light terminates, darkness begins. This suggests day and night on a spherical globe.

Many commentaries try to attribute this verse in Job to Strabo's concept of a flat, disk-shaped earth. From a historical viewpoint, this is impossible. Job was written ages before the writings of Strabo.

The implication of a round earth is seen in the book of Luke, where Jesus described his return, Luke 17:31. Jesus said, "In that day" then in verse 34, "In that night." This is an allusion to light on one side of the globe and darkness on the other simultaneously.

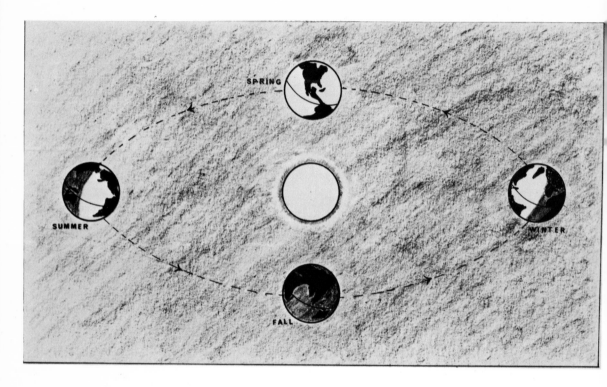

## The earth's seasons

This diagram of the earth's revolution shows the seasons with the spring and autumnal equinoxes. The tilting of the earth is a major factor in producing the seasons. It is no mere accident that the earth is tilted 23.5° so that unequal distribution of solar energy brings about the seasons. The seasons are permanent. "While the earth remaineth, seedtime and harvest, and cold and heat, and summer and winter, and day and night shall not cease" (Genesis 8:22).

The Scripture indicates that it is the work of the Lord in providing day and night and summer and winter. "The day is thine, the night also is thine: thou hast prepared the light [luminaries] and the sun. Thou hast set all the borders of the earth: thou hast made summer and winter" (Psalm 74:16-17).

# 58

# The Earth's Seasons

The seasons are caused primarily by the combined effect of the earth's revolution and the tilt of the earth's axis. God's power and majesty are revealed in the tilting of the earth and the earth's precision in its orbit. The permanence of the season is shown in Genesis 8:22. The axis of the earth is inclined approximately 23.5° from the perpendicular to the ecliptic plane. The tilt causes unequal distribution of the sun's energy; the sun favors the northern hemisphere one-half of the earth's revolution around the sun, and it favors the southern hemisphere for the other half. At the equinox, both hemispheres are equally illuminated. The word *equinox* comes from the Latin *aequi*, meaning "equal," and *nox,* meaning "night". The days and nights are of equal length during the vernal and autumnal equinoxes.

The Hebrews recognized summer as a hot, dry season (Psalm 32:4), and winter as a a rainy season (Song of Solomon 2:11). If rains are adequate, the earth brings forth abundantly as described in Psalm 65:9-13.

> Thou visitest the earth, and waterest it: thou greatly enrichest it with the river of God, which is full of water: thou preparest them corn, when thou hast so provided for it. Thou waterest the ridges thereof abundantly: thou settlest the furrows thereof: thou makest it soft with showers: thou blessest the springing thereof. Thou crownest the year with thy goodness; and thy paths drop fatness. They drop upon the pastures of the wilderness: and the little hills rejoice on every side. The pastures are clothed with flocks; the valleys also are covered over with corn; they shout for joy, they also sing.

# 59

# The Foundations of the Earth

The foundations of the earth appear to make specific reference to the core and mantle of the earth. There is much speculation on the kinds of materials present in the earth. The physical state of such materials at intense pressures and temperatures is not known. The earth's magnetic field tends to support the idea that iron and nickel are present. It is believed that nickel and iron make up a large portion of the materials for a magnetic field.

An attempt has been made to drill a hole in the ocean floor where the crust is separated from the mantle. The crust is separated from the mantle by a zone called the Mohorovicic discontinuity. The project to drill the hole was named Mohole. Mohole was abandoned due to lack of funds, but it has been revived under studies to investigate the spreading of the sea floor.

The secrecy and permanence of the earth's foundations are indicated in Scripture: "Bless the LORD, O my soul. . . . Who laid the foundations of the earth, that it should not be removed for ever" (Psalm 104:1a,5). "Thus saith the LORD; if heaven can be measured, and the foundations of the earth searched out beneath, I will also cast off all the seed of Israel for all that they have done, saith the LORD" (Jeremiah 31:37).

The singing of the stars (Job 38:7) at the laying of the foundations of the earth is frequently interpreted as the noise emitted by actual stars. This does not seem correct, because the poetic nature of Job indicates that the singing of the morning stars and the shouting of the sons of God are a synonymous parallelism. In synonymous parallelisms, the second line repeats the first line except in slightly different words. Thus, the singing stars were the same as the shouting sons of God; both phrases refer to angels (compare Job 1:6 and 2:1-7). Celestial bodies could not have been present at the laying of the foundations of the earth; this is contrary to the sequence of the creation account. Genesis 1 gives the events of creation in chronological order. Chapter 2 merely mentions certain events, but not in order.

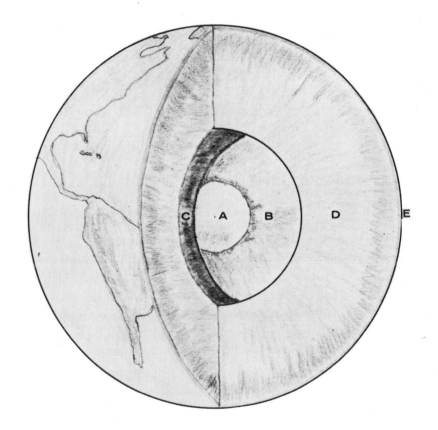

A. inner core
B. outer core
C. boundary of core
D. mantle
E. crust

## The foundations of the earth

A model of the earth's interior based on indirect evidence obtained primarily from seismic data.

"Where wast thou when I laid the foundations of the earth? Declare, if thou hast understanding. Who hath laid the measures [boundaries] thereof, if thou knowest? or who hath stretched the line [measuring line] upon it? Whereupon are the foundations thereof fastened [sunk]? or who laid the corner stone thereof; When the morning stars sang together, and the sons of God shouted for joy?" (Job 38:4-7).

# 60

# The Pillars of the Earth

It is a common belief among some theologians that "the pillars of the earth" mentioned in Scripture refer to a Hebrew superstition that the earth rested on actual pillars, or columns. Those verses which are cited are: 1 Samuel 2:8; Job 9:6, 26:11; Psalm 75:3, and occasionally other verses pertaining to the foundations of the earth. Commentaries have sometimes printed photographs showing the earth being held up by pillars and various other forms of support. Such views are totally foreign to the Scripture.

The Greek word for pillars is *stulos*; the Hebrew word is *ammud*. Both words literally mean columns, but the words may be used in the general sense to mean support, or foundations. The "pillars" mentioned in the New Testament can not readily be misinterpreted, but the word comparable to *pillars* in the Old Testament is frequently misapplied. This may be due to the interpretation of certain passages from the Apocrypha.

In Galatians 2:9, James, Cephas, and John are said to have seemed to be the pillars of the church. This must be interpreted as the main leaders, or the very foundation of the church. The church of the living God is said to be the pillar and ground of truth, 1 Timothy 3:15. This pillar can only mean the foundation of truth. Job 26:11 describes the pillars of heaven as trembling. These are not literal columns but the very basis, or control, of the heavens. In these verses, the word *pillars* could be interchanged with *foundations,* but not with literal columns.

Job 9:6 describes an earthquake in which the pillars (foundations) of the earth are shaken. This implies that the innermost part of the earth undergoes shock waves during the earthquake. In this reference, the pillars may refer to the masses of granitic rock underlying the continents. A similar statement is found in 1 Samuel 2:8 with reference to the pillars of the world. In this reference, "the world" means the habitable part of the earth.

The biblical cosmology is clearly given in Job 26:7, "He hangeth the earth upon nothing." In Scripture, reference to "the pillars of the earth" is frequently used in a general sense as pertaining to anything which gives support or foundation. Reference to "pillars" in Job and the Psalms seems more poetical. In the reference where the meaning is literal, "pillars" refer to the foundations of the earth (or possibly material sunk into the foundations of the earth such as the granitic masses of rock).

The earth is due for another literal shaking during the tribulation period; not only will the earth and heavens be shaken, but the earth will be shaken out of its place. This implies that the orbit is affected.

"Therefore I will shake the heavens, and the earth shall remove out of her place, in the wrath of the LORD of hosts, and in the day of his fierce anger" (Isaiah 13:13).

"For thus saith the LORD of hosts; yet once, it is a little while, and I will shake the heavens, and the earth, and the sea, and the dry land; and I will shake all nations, and the desire of all nations shall come: and I will fill this house with glory, saith the LORD of hosts" (Haggai 2:6-7).

# 61

# The Four Corners of the Earth

Perhaps no phrase in Scripture has been so controversial as the phrase, "the four corners of the earth." The word translated "corners," as in the phrase above, is the Hebrew word, *kanaph. Kanaph* is translated in a variety of ways. However, it generally means extremity. It is translated "borders" in Numbers 15:38. In Ezekiel 7:2 it is translated "four corners" and again in Isaiah 11:12 "four corners;" Job 37:3 and 38:13 as "ends." The Greek equivalent in Revelation 7:1 is *gonia.* The Greek meaning is perhaps more closely related to our modern divisions known as quadrants. *Gonia* literally means angles, or divisions. It is customary to divide a map into quadrants as shown by the four directions.

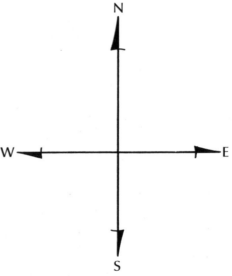

Some have tried to ridicule the Bible to say that it teaches the earth is square. The Scripture makes it quite clear that the earth is a sphere (Isaiah 40:22). Some have tried to say there are four knobs, or peaks on a round earth. Regardless of the various ways *kanaph* is translated, it makes reference to extremities.

There are many ways in which God the Holy Spirit could have said *corner.* Any of the following Hebrew words could have been used: *Pinoh* is used in reference to the cornerstone. *Paioh* means "a geometric corner;" *ziovyoh* means "right angle," or "corner;" and *kmouth* refers to a projecting corner. If the Lord wanted to convey the idea of a square,

### Mountains in the sea

The Mid-Oceanic Ridge is the largest single feature of the earth's crust. This photograph is of a model constructed from oceanographic charts.

"I went down to the bottom of the mountains" (Jonah 2:6).

Underwater photograph by Harold M. Lambert, Philadelphia, Pa.

## The sea

"O LORD, how manifold are thy works! in wisdom hast thou made them all: the earth is full of thy riches. So is this great and wide sea, wherein are things creeping innumerable, both small and great beasts" (Psalm 104:24-25).

four-cornered earth, the Hebrew word *paamouth* could have been used. *Paamouth* means square. Instead, the Holy Spirit selected the word *kanaph,* conveying the idea of extremity.

It is doubtful that any religious Jew would ever misunderstand the true meaning of *kanaph.* For nearly 2,000 years, religious Jews have faced the city of Jerusalem three times daily and chanted the following prayer:

> Sound the great trumpet for our freedom,
> Raise the banner for gathering our exiles,
> And gather us together from the four corners of
> the earth into our own land.

The book of Isaiah describes how the Messiah, the Root of Jesse, shall regather his people from the four corners of the earth. They shall come from every extremity to be regathered in Israel.

> And in that day there shall be a root of Jesse, which shall stand for an ensign of the people; to it shall the Gentiles seek: and his rest shall be glorious. And it shall come to pass in that day, that the Lord shall set his hand again the second time to recover the remnant of his people, which shall be left, from Assyria, and from Egypt, and from Pathros, and from Cush, and from Elam, and from Shinar, and from Hamath, and from the islands of the sea. And he shall set up an ensign for the nations, and shall assemble the outcasts of Israel, and gather together the dispersed of Judah from the *four corners of the earth* (Isaiah 11:10-12, italics added).

## Brimstone and fire on Sodom and Gomorrah

Pictured above is a pinnacle of salt located in the Negev, traditionally called "Lot's wife." "But the same day that Lot went out of Sodom it rained fire and brimstone from heaven, and destroyed them all" (Luke 17:29). "But his wife looked back from behind him, and she became a pillar of salt" (Genesis 19:26).

# 62

# Brimstone and Fire on Sodom and Gomorrah

Most biblical scholars believe the cities of the plain, Sodom, Admah, Gomorrah, Zeboim, and Zoar were located in the southern end of the Dead Sea. The cities of the plain, including Sodom, are believed to be buried beneath the southern part of the sea, possibly at the Lisan Peninsula. Apparently, the cities were not totally under water during ancient times. The historian Josephus referred to the Dead Sea as the Sea of Sodom, indicating its location.

*Baker's Bible Atlas* suggests that petroleum and gases were ignited, causing destruction of these cities. Such an explosion would have caused fire and a mixture of salts to rain down upon the cities. Although this event may involve natural phenomena, Genesis 19:24 specifically states that the brimstone and fire came out of heaven from the Lord.

There is a mountain range known as Jabal Usdum (Mount Sodom) west of the southern end of the Dead Sea. This five-mile long mountain range consists chiefly of crystalline salt formations. There are many free-standing pinnacles of salt that are a living testimony of the destruction of the cities of Sodom and Gomorrah. "And it came to pass, when they had brought them forth abroad, that he said, Escape for thy life; look not behind thee, neither stay thou in all the plain; escape to the mountain, lest thou be consumed. . . . The sun was risen upon the earth when Lot entered into Zoar. Then the LORD rained upon Sodom and upon Gomorrah brimstone and fire from the LORD out of heaven; And he overthrew those cities, and all the plain, and all the inhabitants of the cities, and that which grew upon the ground" (Genesis 19:17, 23-25).

# 63

# The Earth Suspended in Space

The idea of a supported, fixed earth was predominant in early scientific thinking. This was primarily because of the theory proposed by the Egyptian astronomer, Claudius Ptolemaeus (Ptolemy). Ptolemy suggested that the earth was the fixed center of the solar system and that heavenly bodies, such as stars and planets, revolved around it. This concept of a fixed earth continued until the sixteenth century.

In 1543, Nicolous Copernicus, a Polish astronomer, published his theory on the motion of planetary bodies and rotation of the earth. The work of Copernicus, along with that of Sir Isaac Newton, forms the basis of most of our modern concepts of planetary motion. The work of Copernicus supported the view of a spherical earth as well as rotation of the earth. Copernicus gave detailed explanations on the earth's revolution around the sun. The views of Ptolemy were deeply rooted into the religious leaders of that time, and the Copernican theory received great opposition.

Sir Isaac Newton (1642-1727) published the laws of gravitation and provided an explanation for the fact that the earth is suspended in space, held by its attraction to the sun. The Bible clearly states that the earth hangs on nothing (Job 26:7).

The law of gravitation states that every particle of matter in the universe attracts every other particle with a force that varies directly as the product of their masses and inversely as the square of the distance between them. By this law, motions of celestial bodies can be calculated and future motions predicted. God has established these physical laws that govern the universe, but He is the ultimate Sustainer and Power that controls these laws. "Upholding all things by the word of his power" (Hebrews 1:3b).

# 64

# Isostasy

Seismic data indicates that there is an equilibrium maintained within the earth's crust. This equilibrium, or balance in the earth's crust is called isostasy, which means "equal standing." Data compiled from volcanoes, earthquakes, and underground nuclear explosions support the idea of equilibrium within the earth's crust. The exact mechanism whereby this equilibrium is maintained is not understood.

Seismic data indicates that perhaps as much as 95 percent of the continental volume may be granite. Some scientists think the granitic masses "float" on top of basalt. Still others maintain that the granitic masses are situated in sockets down into the mantle of the earth and the plastic flow of rocks may be some other type of material. There are various modifications of this theory. According to the most commonly accepted view, the lighter granitic materials of the earth's crust rise higher than the denser basalt. If some area of the crust is weighted down under pressure and it sinks, another part will rise higher to offset this shift. If the theory of isostasy is correct, removal of oil and natural resources should cause more earthquakes.

Balance does exist in the earth's crust, but none of the current theories adequately explains the isostatic balance. In all probability, the mechanism of equilibrium within the earth's crust involves forces and materials totally unknown to man at this time. Hundreds of years before the science of geophysics suggested this balance in the earth's crust, God implied that He was responsible for this isostatic balance (Isaiah 40:12).

## Camels near the Dead Sea

"The waters shall be healed" (Ezekiel 47:8*b*).

# 65

# An Earthquake, and the Dead Sea Becomes a Living Sea

The Dead Sea is in the middle of the geological fault which runs from Mount Hermon through the Gulf of Aqabah. It is located at the lowest point of this great fault, situated at 1,292 feet below sea level. The Jordan River flows into the Dead Sea, but there is no outlet for water except through evaporation. Heat, evaporation, and the flow of fresh water into the sea cause variation in the salt content. It is approximately six times saltier than ocean water. Animal life cannot exist in the water; fish would float because of the buoyancy of salt water.

Studies of the Dead Sea indicate that where the Jordan flows into the Dead Sea, there are zones of sweet water flowing into the salt water. Studies of the microflora of the Dead Sea by Benjamin Elazari-Volcani indicate that there are two general types of bacteria that can survive in these waters: bacteria known as halophiles, which require salt, and halotolerant ones, which will tolerate a fairly high concentration of salt. Except for these microorganisms, the Dead Sea is truly dead.

Dead Sea waters are rich in potassium chloride, magnesium chloride, and calcium chloride; these salts are extracted and exported. Magnesium chloride gives the water a nasty taste; calcium chloride gives it a slick feeling. The strong concentration of salts gives great buoyancy but inhibits life. In addition to the salts, asphalt floats ashore. The historian Josephus called it the Sea of Asphalt and the Sea of Sodom. It is called the salt sea in Numbers 34:3, 12 and Deuteronomy 3:17.

During the Millennium, the Dead Sea waters are to be healed following an earthquake. Fish will be restored as waters issue out from the temple in Jerusalem and flow through the Dead Sea (Ezekiel 47:8-10). It will be a living sea with an abundance of fish like the Great Sea, the Mediterranean

147

Photograph by Matson Photo Service, Alhambra, Calif. (Alterations on photograph made by author).

### The Mount of Olives shall cleave in half.

"And his feet shall stand in that day upon the mount of Olives, which is before Jerusalem on the east, and the mount of Olives shall cleave in the midst thereof toward the east and toward the west, and there shall be a very great valley; and half of the mountain shall remove toward the north, and half of it toward the south. . . . And the LORD shall be king over all the earth: in that day shall there be one LORD, and his name one (Zechariah 14:4,9).

The representation of the Mount of Olives cleaving in half is highly diagrammatic. Although there are valleys and faulting in this area, no specific spot can be marked as the cleavage point.

148

(Ezekiel 47:10). Half the waters from the temple in Jerusalem will go east into the Dead Sea and the other half will flow west into the Mediterranean (Zechariah 14:8). The entire lay of the land must be altered by the earthquake, as shown in Zechariah 14:10, where it says all the land shall be turned like a plain.

> All the land shall be turned as a plain from Geba to Rimmon south of Jerusalem: and it shall be lifted up, and inhabited in her place, from Benjamin's gate unto the place of the first gate, unto the corner gate, and from the tower of Hananeel unto the king's winepresses (Zechariah 14:10).
>
> Then said he unto me, these waters issue out toward the east country, and go down into the desert, and go into the sea: which being brought forth into the sea, the waters shall be healed. And it shall come to pass, that every thing that liveth, which moveth, whithersoever the rivers shall come, shall live: and there shall be a very great multitude of fish, because these waters shall come thither: for they shall be healed; every thing shall live whither the river cometh. And it shall come to pass, that the fishers shall stand upon it from Engedi even unto Eneglaim; they shall be a place to spread forth nets; their fish shall be according to their kinds, as the fish of the great sea [the Mediterranean], exceedingly many. (Ezekiel 47:8-10).

The earthquake that separates the Mount of Olives is indicated in Zechariah 14:4-10. The Mount shall cleave in half from east to west; one half is removed toward the south, the other toward the north. The Dead Sea must lift up to sea level, for fresh water from it will flow into the Red Sea.

Earthquakes follow fault lines. In the Holy Land, however, the fault lines are extremely complex. Large fault lines run from northeast to southwest. The Jordan Rift runs from north to south. The fault lines and the rift are imposed upon each other. In addition, cross fault lines run northwest to southeast and west to east.

# VI

# ZOOLOGY

Photograph by Harold M. Lambert, Philadelphia, Pa.

"For every beast of the forest is mine, and the cattle upon a thousand hills.

"I know all the fowls of the mountains; and the wild beasts of the field are mine . . .

"But ask now the beasts, and they shall teach thee; and the fowls of the air, and they shall tell thee:

"Or speak to the earth, and it shall teach thee: and the fishes of the sea shall declare unto thee.

"Who knoweth not in all these that the hand of the LORD hath wrought this?

"In whose hand is the soul of every living thing, and the breath of all mankind" (Psalm 50:10-11; Job 12:7-10).

# 66

# Animals of the Bible

This section on zoology is not an exhaustive study of the animals of the Bible. It is undertaken with the idea of pointing out a few of the unique characteristics of the biblical animals that show God's hand in nature. In addition, it is an effort to discuss some of the animals whose names have been mistranslated. The Bible is sometimes subjected to harsh criticism because of the mistranslated animal names. An attempt to compile some information on snakes that has been omitted from most other previous publications on biblical animals has been made here also.

Some of the animals of the Bible are mentioned or described in the poetical books. Six of the books of the Bible; Job, Psalms, Proverbs, Ecclesiastes, Song of Solomon, and Lamentations, are mostly Hebraic poetry. The poetic descriptions of the animals contain figures of speech such as similies, hyperboles and metaphors. These are especially noticeable in the book of Job. One of the animals in Job is said to drink up a river. This figure of speech is used to convey the idea of the enormous amount of water that can be consumed by that animal. Psalm 119:136, "Rivers of water run down mine eyes." Both the statement in Job and that in Psalm 119 have been considered as errors by some. Neither is an error; they are figures of speech.

Animal identifications presented here are based on *Ha-Millon He-Chadash* (New Dictionary) by Even-Shoshan, Jerusalem, 1975 and from *List of the Animals Mentioned in the Bible* by Professor A. Shulov, The Jerusalem Biblical Zoo, 1975.

# 67

# Classification of Living Things

Before discussing animals of the Bible, it seems necessary to point out the differences in classification systems. Animals are classified in Scripture according to simple characteristics that give quick recognition. For example, animals are classified as creeping, crawling, flying, and so forth. Man classifies animals on the basis of what he terms an evolutionary scale. This is based chiefly on detailed external features; little attention is paid to the chemical complexity of most animals.

In Scripture, the bat is listed with things that fly, like the bird. This is a quick way of identification for any observer. Modern man classifies the bat with the mammals because it has mammary glands and gives bat milk.

A similar situation is found in the grouping or classification of the hyrax and hare (Leviticus 11:5-6), with animals that chew the cud. Both the hyrax and hare chew a great deal, but they do not have the three or four-chambered stomach of a ruminant. According to man's classification, a cud-chewer has a three- or four-chambered stomach and must bring up the material from the first stomach and re-chew it. For a quick reference, the hare and hyrax are classified with the cud-chewers of the Bible because they give the appearance of cud-chewing. In addition to this, God classes them with the cud-chewers because they have a chemical process of cellulose decomposition that is like rumination. This is a fact that man did not know until thousands of years later.

The Hebrew word *gerah* is rendered as "chewing the cud" in most translations. The exact meaning of *gerah* cannot be determined. Many Orthodox Jews consider it a second mastication, or the semblance of chewing. (For further discussion, see sections on the hare and hyrax.)

A similar problem of classification is encountered in the "kinds" of Genesis. The "kinds" mentioned in Genesis are those plants or animals that do not interbreed. *Kinds* sometimes refers to what modern man calls

154

'genus" (plural genera); in other cases *kind* means "family." In some instances, *kinds* refers to the species. Most genera do not interbreed with other genera, but there are exceptions to this rule. Similar species will sometimes interbreed. For example, the domesticated cat, *Felis catus* will cross with the wildcat. The wildcat and the domesticated cat belong to the same genus, but they are different species. (*Simba* by C. A. W. Guggisberg.)

In some cases, however, genera can interbreed. A classic example of crosses between genera is seen in the grasses that will mix with certain cereal grains. *Kinds* in Genesis could not apply to these genera, because they can interbreed. Here *kinds* most likely would be the equivalent of *family*. The horse and donkey belong to the same genus, but they are different species. When mated, the resulting mule is sterile. Since the offspring is sterile, it appears that the species is the near limit of the kinds. The rabbis considered the horse and donkey as diverse kinds and would not interbreed them (see Leviticus 19:19).

It is obvious that the "kinds" of Genesis do not fit man's classification system. Furthermore, throughout Scripture it is impossible to fit God's method of classication into that of man's. "For my thoughts are not your thoughts, neither are your ways my ways, saith the Lord. For as the heavens are higher than the earth, so are my ways higher than your ways, and my thoughts than your thoughts" (Isaiah 55:8-9).

## A male wild goat in its habitat

"Knowest thou the time when the wild goats of the rock bring forth? Or canst thou mark when the hinds do calve? Canst thou number the months that they fulfill? Or knowest thou the time when they bring forth? They bow themselves, they bring forth their young ones, they cast out their sorrows. Their young ones are in good liking, they grow up with corn; they go forth, and return not unto them" (Job 39:1-4).

# 68

# The Wild Goats

The wild goat of the Bible is called the Nubian ibex. Its scientific name is *Capra ibex nubiana.* The wild goat is indigenous to the Holy Land. Wild goats live primarily in the Afro-Syrian Rift between the Dead Sea and the Red Sea. They prefer the crags and rocks of cliffs, as described in the Bible. David fled from Saul along the Dead Sea to En Gedi; this is called "the rocks of the wild goats" (1 Samuel 24:2). The goats prefer the rocky cliffs; "The high hills are a refuge for the wild goats" (Psalm 104:18).

During Job's oral examination, he was asked questions about wild goats. In Job 39:1, Job was asked whether he could regulate the birth of wild goats. It is God who regulates the laws of nature. The thought here is not that their birth is of a secretive nature, but a factor of design by the Creator who regulates the laws of nature. In verse 1, the use of the word *hind* generally is applied to the female gazelle or deer. In this context, however, it refers to the female wild goat. In verse 2, God asked Job if he could regulate the period of gestation. Obviously it is the Creator who regulates these things. Verse 3 describes how the wild goats give birth to their young. In verse 4, "Their young ones are in good liking," means they develop rapidly, and they eat grain early in their development.

The Nubian ibex is protected by the Nature Reserves Authority of Israel. There are at present about 2,000 goats in Israel. They live in herds of a few goats, usually about eight or ten. It seems to be significant that the Hebrew word *yé elim* is in the plural; perhaps this makes reference to their nature of remaining in herds.

Drawing by Alen Edgar, College Park, Md.

## The Syrian wild ass

The Syrian wild ass and the Persian wild ass resemble one another. The markings and color are slightly different. In Job's examination, the Lord questions Job about the wild ass. Could Job provide this wild creature with such unusual characteristics? Note the use of the Hebrew *arod* for the Persian wild ass and *pere* for the Syrian wild ass.

"Who hath sent out the wild ass [pere] free? Or who hath loosed the bands of the wild ass [arod]? Whose house I have made the wilderness, and the barren land his dwellings. He scorneth the multitude of the city, neither regardeth he the crying of the driver. The range of the mountains is his pasture, and he searcheth after every green thing" (Job 39:5-8).

158

# 69

# The Wild Ass

There are two Hebrew words in Scripture which are rendered "wild ass;" they are *pere* and *arod*. The Jerusalem Biblical Zoo identifies the Hebrew *arod* as the Persian wild ass, *Equus hemionus onager*; the Hebrew *pere*, is identified as the Syrian wild ass known as *Equus hemionus hemippus*. The Syrian wild ass is extinct; the last one was reported to have been seen in the early 1900's. The Persian wild ass still exists but is in danger of extinction.

In Job's oral examination, the wild ass is indicative of God's loving care for the things of nature. The ass made his home in the wilderness; he didn't have a barn. The barren land was his dwelling (Job 39:6). The wild ass avoided the inhabited places and did not obey the driver like the domesticated ass (v. 7). God had provided pasture and equipped it for living in the wilderness (v. 8). Could Job do such a spectacular thing, creating nature with such diversity?

God compared the nation of Israel to a swift Arabian camel, the dromedary. The nation turned after other gods (Baalism). The nation was so untamable that she is compared to a wild ass in heat. "Thou art a swift dromedary traversing her ways; a wild ass used to the wilderness, that snuffeth up the wind at her pleasure; in her occasion who can turn her away? All they that seek her will not weary themselves; in her month they shall find her" (Jeremiah 2:23b & 24). God so carefully guided the nation of Israel, but she so swiftly turned away, time after time. (See Jeremiah 2:20-21.)

Drawing by Alen Edgar, College Park, Md. The biblical wild ox is copied from the American Museum of Natural History, by permission. Drawing is altered to agree with ancient sculpture.

## The biblical wild ox

Job is asked whether the wild ox could be trusted to plow and harrow the fields. Could the sowing of seed and gathering of the harvest be left to him? The wild ox was noted for its strength, but the wild nature that the Creator had bestowed upon him did not make him suitable for work like the domesticated ox.

"Will the unicorn [wild ox] be willing to serve thee, or abide by thy crib? Canst thou bind the unicorn [wild ox] with his band in the furrow? Or will he harrow the valleys after thee? Wilt thou trust him, because his strength is great? Or wilt thou leave thy labor to him? Wilt thou believe him, that he will bring home thy seed, and gather it into thy barn" (Job 39:9-12).

# 70

# The Wild Ox

The Hebrew word *re'em* has been translated *unicorn, rhinoceros, oryx,* and a variety of other terms. The wild ox can be identified by its Assyrian name *rimu*, which is equivalent to the German *auroch*. *Re'em* is rendered *unicorn* in the King James Version, but this has no sound basis. The unicorn is a one-horned, mythological character. The horns of *re'em* are plural in Deuteronomy 33:17, and the word *wild ox* should be singular, rather than the plural *unicorns*. (See the 1901 ASV for the proper rendering of this verse.)

The biblical wild ox was *Bos primigenius,* a now extinct species. The last living specimen was reported in Europe during the early 1600's. In ancient times, the wild ox was portrayed in frescoes and in Assyrian sculpture. In most ancient artwork, it was portrayed as a large, stocky ox, much larger than the domesticated one. It is rather heavy through the shoulders. Its horns come forward, then up; whereas the domesticated ox has horns that come out more to the sides, then forward.

The biblical wild ox, known by its German name, *aurochs,* was also called by a variety of terms such as *ur, uri, urus, aur,* and *uru.* These terms were derived from the German or Latinized form of the name. The Germans have attempted to recapture this creature by a series of back-breeding experiments. There is a herd in Munich, Germany that was obtained by back-breeding; the oxen resemble the characteristics of the ancient wild ox.

The wild ox is mentioned in Deuteronomy 33:17, in regard to the blessings of Moses upon the children of Israel; of Joseph he said "The firstling of his herd, majesty is his; and his horns are the horns of the wild ox" (ASV).

## The male ostrich

Notice the large, powerful legs and the beautiful white wing quills that are characteristic of the males.

# 71

# The Ostrich

The Syrian ostrich inhabited the deserts of Israel and Sinai until the 1940's when it was extirpated. Presently, the ostrich inhabits Africa and Arabia.

The natural habitat of the ostrich is the desert or savanna. It is often compared to the camel from which it derives its Latinized name, *Struthio camelus,* which means ostrich camel. Although its habitat is the desert or savanna, it must remain fairly close to an oasis containing water. It drinks about a gallon and a half of water a day. The ostrich lives mainly on a diet of vegetation, but will also consume animals; it is omnivorous. Its taste ranges from baby snakes to shiny coins. It has a ravenous appetite and will avidly devour bright metallic objects. In captivity, almost any object may be found in the crop of an ostrich.

The ostrich is the largest of all living birds. An ostrich grows to a height of about eight feet, and the male can weigh up to 350 pounds. Its legs are very powerful, and it can run approximately 25 to 35 miles an hour. The birds are often seen using their wings to get started or to slow down.

The males and females can be distinguished by color. The males are black with white quills on the wings and white tail coverts. The hens are brownish-grey and not quite as large as the cocks. There is great variability in behavior, but the general pattern of rearing their young is about the same in all races of ostriches.

The ostrich is polygamous, and several hens use the same nest for laying their eggs. The cock digs out a nest in the sand. The nest is about one foot deep and three feet across. It takes forty-two days for the eggs to hatch. Both hens and cock take turns incubating the eggs until they hatch. The ostrich must sit on the eggs at night because it gets cold in the desert regions. During the day, the eggs may be left alone in the warm sand. That is the meaning of Job 39:14, "Which leaveth her eggs in the earth,

163

and warmeth them in the dust." It should be noted that some varieties of the ostrich behave somewhat differently in the wild. Sometimes a head hen drives other hens away and sits on the nest mostly in the day. Because of the warm sand, she can leave the nest at random. The male incubates mostly at night.

Photographed from an exhibit at the Natural History Museum, courtesy of the Smithsonian Institution, Washington, D.C.

## Ostrich chicks

Note the eggs which have failed to hatch; these have been carelessly left on the ground.

"[The ostrich] which leaveth her eggs in the earth, and warmeth them in the dust, and forgetteth that the foot may crush them, or that the wild beast may break them. She is hardened against her young ones, as though they were not hers; her labor is in vain without fear" (Job 39:14-16).

164

The Hebrew words, *ya-en* and *ya'anah* refer to the ostrich. The word translated *peacock* in the King James Version in Job 39:13 is the word that refers to the ostrich hen. Unfortunately the word translated *ostrich* in that same verse is the Hebrew word *chasidah,* meaning stork. Some commentaries consider the word an error in transcription. This does not seem to be an error in transcription but a beautiful comparison between the cruelty of the ostrich and the loving-kindness of the stork. The following rendering of the verse changes both words: "The wings of the ostrich beateth proudly; but are they the pinions and feathers of the kindly stork's?" (Job 39:13, author's translation).

The Revised Standard Version translates the word for *stork* as *love.* It says, "Are they the plumage of love?" This does not convey the idea that a bird is intended in the context. The Hebrew word *chasidah* is used in this verse. It is derived from the noun *chesed,* meaning loving-kindness. This is the name given to the stork in Hebrew literature. The stork is kindly and very attentive to her young, a characteristic that is somewhat lacking in the ostrich hen but partially supplied by the cock. It is the cock that aids in incubation of the eggs, and he takes charge of the chicks.

Job 39:14 states that she leaves her eggs in the earth to be warmed in the dust. As previously mentioned, it is the cock who digs the hole for the nest. As the hens share the nest, most of the eggs are covered with sand, but a few are carelessly left out from under the sand. These uncovered eggs get broken and later provide the nourishment for the newly hatched chicks. God uses her stupidity to provide food for the young.

The ostrich is cruel because she forgets that a beast can trample her eggs (v. 15). Ostrich eggs have a tough shell and are not readily broken, but the heavy foot of an animal can crush them. The oryx (antelope) is reported to eat the eggs. "She is hardened against her young ones," meaning the unhatched eggs (v. 16). All the effort of sitting on the eggs for forty-two days is in vain if they are smashed. Her lack of understanding refers to her lack of motherly love (v. 17). She does not display the usual motherly instincts of most wild birds or domesticated fowl for eggs and chicks.

The ostrich may lack wisdom, but she can outrun the horse and his rider. This is why it states that she scorns the horse and his rider in Job 39:18. All these diverse characteristics display creative design. Obviously, Job must have been overwhelmed by the knowledge displayed by the Creator.

# 72

# The Stork

The stork is mentioned by its Hebrew name *chasidah,* which is translated "ostrich" in the King James Version (Job 39:13). The stork is called kind because of its motherly love toward its young, and because of its ability to get along with other birds. The Hebrew word *chasidah,* is derived from the root word *chesed,* meaning "loving-kindness."

The stork does not normally hatch its eggs in Israel. The stork is a migrant that passes through Israel in the fall and spring as it travels from Eastern Europe to North Africa.

Photograph by Wolfe Worldwide Films, Los Angeles, Calif.

## The stork

The stork *Ciconia ciconia* nesting in an abandoned chimney in Morocco.

According to Psalm 104:16-17, the stork nests in Lebanon. There are indications that the fir trees in this psalm may have been the juniper trees, "as for the stork, the fir trees are her house" (Psalm 104:17*b*).

Bird migrations were recognized by the prophet Jeremiah, and he mentioned the stork's appointed time of migration. "Yea, the stork in heaven knoweth her appointed times; and the turtle [turtledove] and the crane and the swallow observe the time of their coming; but my people know not the judgment of the LORD" (Jeremiah 8:7).

Photograph by Harold M. Lambert, Philadelphia, Pa.

## The great river hippopotamus

Behold now behemoth, which I made [created] with thee; he eateth
grass as an ox. Lo now, his strength is in his loins, and his force is in the
navel of his belly [his sinews and muscles] (Job 40:15-16).

For identification of behemoth as the hippopotamus, see: *List of the
Animals Mentioned in the Bible* by Professor A. Shulov, The Jerusalem
Biblical Zoo, 1975.

# 73

# The Hippopotamus

The word rendered *behemoth* in the King James Version in Job 40:15 is the intensive plural of the Hebrew *behemah,* meaning beast. The Jerusalem Biblical Zoo defines *behemoth* as the hippopotamus. This seems correct, based on the biological description found in Job. The creature has very real characteristics, not mythological ones. In addition, some rabbinical writings identify this beast as the hippopotamus. *Behemoth* has been considered as denoting an elephant by some writers. This is based on the word *swords,* which refers to eyeteeth. But it should be noted that the hippopotamus has large, tusk-like eyeteeth.* Other characteristics are nearer the hippopotamus than the elephant. Verses 20 through 23 seem to rule out the elephant as a possibility.

The behemoth is a real animal that eats grass like an ox; has an aquatic-like life in the marshes and likes to lie under shade trees. According to the *Encyclopedia Judaica,* the hippopotamus once lived in the area of the Yarkon River.

The original interpretation of *leviathan* and *behemoth* as mythological characters stems from the Talmudic interpretation. Their mythological interpretation has no sound theological basis, and many Jewish rabbis interpret these animals as the crocodile and hippopotamus. Job is asked forty-two scientific questions in the last few chapters of Job. The questions cover astronomy, geology, biology, and various other topics. A careful analysis of these questions will reveal that they refer to real phenomena of creation. Other animals included in Job's examination were the hawk, the lion, the raven, the wild goat, the wild ass, the wild ox, the ostrich, and the eagle (griffon vulture). The wild ox was listed, in the

*Low-grade ivory is obtained from the tusk of a hippopotamus.

KJV, under the name of a mythological character, the unicorn, but this is an error in translation; it should be translated "wild ox." All other animals mentioned in Job are real; it is therefore logical to assume that the behemoth and leviathan are real animals.

"Behold now behemoth, which I made with thee," refers to the fact that God created both the behemoth and Job. "He eats grass like an ox" (Job 40:15). The hippopotamus is herbivorous. "His strength is in his loins" (v. 16). The hippopotamus weighs about 6,000 pounds, and much of his weight and strength are concentrated in his abdominal region. The reference is to the great river hippopotamus known as *Hippopotamus amphibius*. "His force is in the naval of his belly," is rendered as the force being in his stays, which means in his muscles. "His tail is like a cedar" (v. 17), is a simile. This describes how the hippopotamus holds his tail when he runs or is frightened. "The sinews of his stones [thighs]" (v. 17), refer to his great strength. Verse 18 makes reference to the strength of his bones.

He is a strong animal that only God should encounter. "He [the Creator] that made him can make his sword" (v. 19). This refers to his large eyeteeth. The thought here is that the Creator can approach him, but no one else had better try. Verse 19 has caused some to consider this animal an elephant, but verse 23 and 24 seem to rule this out. The species name of the hippopotamus is *amphibius*. This refers to his nature of staying in the water part of the day and coming out to eat on dry land in the night (v. 20). He may also seek food from the surrounding hills. The word *mountains* in this text can also be used to mean hills. The beasts of the field play around him because he is not carnivorous; he is herbivorous (v. 20). He has a marsh habitat of shady trees, reeds, and fens (v. 21-22).

Verses 23 and 24 are quoted from the American Standard Version, 1901. The King James is not clear on these verses: "Behold, if a river overflow, he trembleth not; He is confident, though a Jordan swell even to his mouth. Shall any take him when he is on the watch, or pierce through his nose with a snare?"

He is not afraid even though a Jordan rushes forth to his mouth (v. 23). The hippopotamus far surpasses the elephant in its ability to handle itself in a rising stream. This verse rules out the elephant. An elephant enjoys water but, he is not amphibious. The use of the article *a* implies a very swift stream which comes up to the creature's mouth. The hippopotamus is alert; he is on the watch (v. 24).

The forty-two scientific questions in these last few chapters of Job refer to real phenomena of creation. The hippopotamus is no exception to the rule. Fossil remains along the delta of the Nile verify that the hippopotamus existed in lower Egypt. Frescoes and writings also testify to this fact. The entire thought expressed throughout Job's interrogation is whether Job could display or perform such marvelous acts of creation. Could Job create an animal with such diverse characteristics as the hippopotamus?

"Then Job answered the LORD, and said, I know that thou canst do every thing, and that no thought can be withholden from thee. . . . Therefore have I uttered that I understood not; things too wonderful for me which I knew not" (Job 42:1-3).

# 74

# The Crocodile

The description of the *leviathan* in Job 41:1 fits the Nile crocodile, *Crocodilus niloticus*. The creature described in Job has characteristics such as scales, thick armor, teeth, strong jaws, and a fierce nature. The leviathan is sometimes considered a mythological character, as is the behemoth. The description would not be meaningful if it were mythological; the questions asked Job refer to phenomena of creation.

The word *leviathan* in modern Hebrew usage means whale. When *leviathan* is used in Job, it cannot mean *whale,* because whales do not fit the description of Job 41:13-17. The animal described there has terrible teeth, scales, thick armor, powerful jaws, and a fierce nature. There are two types of whales. One has no teeth and uses its mouth to strain plankton; the other type has teeth. The similarity between a whale and the animal described in Job 41 stops with the teeth. Whales do not have scales, a thick armor, or a fierce nature.

The Nile crocodile once lived in Israel; the river Nahal ha-Taninim in Sharon was named for it. Just outside of the Nahal Taninim Reserve is the Tell of Crocodilopolis, the ancient city of crocodiles. The crocodile inhabited the Egyptian part of the Nile until the ninteenth century when it was extirpated; it is indigenous to Africa.

The beginning of chapter 41 is somewhat ironic. Verses 1 and 2 ask if the crocodile would be treated like a fish when it is caught. It was customary to put a rope (ring of rushes) through the gills or nose of a fish. "Canst thou put a rope into his nose?" (v. 2, ASV). Verse 3 is also ironical of his ferocious nature, "will he speak soft words?" (v. 4, ASV). A crocodile cannot be made a servant like a domesticated animal, "wilt thou take him for a servant for ever?" (v. 4, KJV).

"Wilt thou play with him as with a bird?" (v. 5) may refer to the little crocodile bird that fearlessly picks leeches from the crocodile. There are

Drawing by Alen Edgar, College Park, Md.

## Nile crocodile

"Wilt thou play with him as with a bird?" (Job 41:5a).

The Nile crocodile, *Crocodilus niloticus,* with a bird cleaning the leeches off him. For identification of Leviathan as the crocodile *see Ha-Millon He-Chadash* (The New Dictionary) by A. Even-Shoshan, Jerusalem 1975, Kyrat-Sepher Publisher, page 1464.

Photograph—Apollo 17 view of the earth. Courtesy of National Aeronautics and Space Administration, Washington, D.C.

## The earth suspended in space

The Scripture explicitly states that the earth hangs on nothing. This implies gravitational attraction. This biblical cosmology was recorded thousands of years before scientists ever suggested such a scientific concept. "He stretcheth out the north over the empty place, and hangeth the earth upon nothing" (Job 26:7).

Photograph by Jeffrey Watson, Washington Bible College, Lanham, Md.

## Isostasy

Isostasy is the balance in the earth's crust. Hundreds, even thousands of years before geophysicists suggested such a scientific concept, God indicated that He is responsible for this delicate balance between land masses and water of the earth. "Who hath measured the waters in the hollow of his hand, and meted out heaven with the span, and comprehended the dust of the earth in a measure, and weighed the mountains in scales, and the hills in a balance?" (Isaiah 40:12).

174

reports that it will even pick the teeth of the crocodile. (See *Animal Life and Lore* by Osmond Breland.) The Egyptian plover, *Pluvianus aegyptius,* is the bird that feasts on the leeches from the crocodile. It closely resembles the sandpiper.

The crocodile was sacred in certain parts of Egypt. It was eaten in Elephantine and Appollonopolis in spite of its sacredness elsewhere. Apparently it was salted and eaten like saltfish. This appears to be the meaning of verse 6. A similar situation is seen in Psalm 74:13-14, where it is said to have been eaten in the wilderness: "Thou didst divide the sea by thy strength: thou brakest the heads of the dragons [*tannim,* crocodiles] in the waters. Thou brakest the heads of leviathan [crocodile] in pieces, and gavest him to be meat to the people inhabiting the wilderness." These verses are parallel and should be considered together. In Psalm 74:13, *tannim* refers to the crocodile, and so does leviathan in verse 14.

Job 41:7 refers to the custom of harpooning the crocodile; verse 8 gives instructions about not placing hands on him. It is hopeless to think of conquering him; the very sight of him is sufficient (v. 9). No one dares stir him up; the crocodile is fierce (v. 10). Over 1,000 women and children are eaten each year, (reported by Gerald Wood in *Animal Facts and Feats*, New York: Doubleday, 1972, pg. 172). If no one is able to stand before this creature which God created, how can he stand before God (v. 10)? Everything belongs to God, even leviathan (v. 11). Verse 12 describes the limbs; verse 13 describes his armor of scales as impenetrable. His double bridle is his extremely powerful jaws. "His teeth are terrible round about" refers to his interlocking teeth that never miss a bite (v. 14). Verses 15 through 17 explain how good and protective the crocodile's armor of scales is.

The reference to smoke and fire in verses 20 and 21 has caused some to interpret this chapter as meaning a dragon or mythological character. This reference is purely poetical. The book of Job is filled with similies, hyperboles, and metaphors in its description of animals. Verses 18 through 21 refer to the habit of the crocodile in spraying a forceful stream of water from his nose. The nostrils are covered with flap-like coverings. The crocodile snorts these valves open, giving a blast of spray. This spray is beautifully described as a boiling pot as it appears as he plunges through the water (v. 20). In context, these four verses appear as metaphorical expressions that are closely allied to the poetical expression of the boiling pot in verse 20. The crocodile expels a forceful spray as he plunges through the water. His sneezing and snorting brings forth glistening and shining spray in the sunlight.

In Egyptian hieroglyphs, the eye of the crocodile represented the dawn. "The eyelids of the morning" appears to be a similar figurative statement (v. 18). The eyes are covered with a thin membrane. The crocodile floats under water, so that all one can see are his nose and the faint glow of his eyes.

Verse 22 refers to the intense strength of the neck; verse 23 describes his firm muscles; verse 24 describes his heart as the "nether millstone" that bears most of the pressure. Anyone is terrified when he rises up (v. 24).

The crocodile swallows large stones that stay in its stomach and counterbalance the floating effect of his lungs. The rocks help him counterbalance himself in order that he can float silently just beneath the surface of the water. The crocodile is able to lunge forward with great force, either in the water or on the land.

Few weapons are effective against him (vv. 26-29). "Sharp stones" literally means "sharp potsherds," or fragments of pottery on which writing or imprints are made (v. 30). This reference means the crocodile makes an imprint in the mud, as though it had been pounded with a threshing sledge. He leaves a foaming, glistening mixture in his pathway because of the churning action of his powerful tail (vv. 31-35). He is king of beasts (vv. 33-34).

# 75

# Seed-harvesting Ants

The ant in Scripture is called by the Hebrew word *nemalah* from the verb *namal,* which means "to cut off." This most likely refers to its habit of cutting off seeds. The ants in Proverbs are the seed-harvesting ants belonging to the genus *Messor.* They are quite similar to the American harvester ant found in the great plains.

Entomologists did not believe there were such things as seed-harvesting ants in the Mediterranean until the ants were investigated by J. T. Moggridge of Europe and Henry McCook of America in 1880. Several ancient writings, including the Bible, mentioned the seed-harvesting ants, but entomologists thought the ants to be purely fictitious.

Seed-harvesting ants prepare their food during the summer just as the Scripture says they do. They cut off seeds of wild or cultivated grasses and have been known to gather seeds from as many as eighteen plant families. The worker ant cuts the seed off and delivers it to the door, where another ant takes the seed and bites off the chaff. It also bites out the germ end to keep the seed from germinating in the damp, underground storage bins. When food is scarce, the ants use seed from the underground granary.

During the winter months, the ants check the grain; if any of it is germinating, the grain is eaten or removed. The seeds are ground by certain ants with very large mandibles. Spittle is mixed with the starchy flour. The enzymes in the spittle cause the starch to be converted to sugar. This results in a sticky dough that is commonly called "ant biscuits." The workers eat after they feed the queen and the larvae.

Harvester ants are only one type of these strange little creatures. There are carpenter, mason, miner, engineer, builder, farmer, doctor, nurse, and sanitary engineer ants.

In Proverbs we are admonished to be wise like the ant, who industriously puts away her food in the summer. A remarkable scientific statement is made in Proverbs 6:7. It states that the ants do not have a guide, overseer, or ruler. The workers do not have a leader comparable to that of other groups of animals. Ants secrete hormones that make the trail and provide a colony odor. These hormones direct most of the colony activities. Note the detailed scientific accuracy implied by the statement in Proverbs.

Some time around 1,000 B.C., Solomon said that the ant prepared her meat, or food in summer. Man did not believe this and did not discover the harvesting ants in Palestine until the 1880's, although these ants were known to exist in other parts of the world.

"Go to the ant, thou sluggard; consider her ways and be wise: which having no guide or overseer, or ruler, provideth her meat in the summer, and gathereth her food in the harvest" (Proverbs 6:6-8).

"The ants are a people not strong, yet they prepare their meat in the summer" (Proverbs 30:25).

# 76

# The Hare

The Hebrew word *arnebeth* is translated "hare" in the King James Version. This seems to be the proper identification of the animal called *arnebeth*. The Scofield Reference Bible states this is not the hare but an unidentified animal. The Hebrew word *arnebeth* is associated with the Akkadian *annabu,* meaning the jumper. Furthermore, the Latin Vulgate translates hare by its genus name, *Lepus.* The Talmud gives still further evidence that *arnebeth* is the hare. The arnebeth has been consistently identified by Orthodox Jews as the hare. *Arnebeth* has further been verified by the Jerusalem Biblical Zoo as the hare. Scofield's footnotes on *arnebeth* have no sound etymological basis.

There are two common species of hares in the Holy Land— *Lepus syriacus* and *Lepus aegyptiacus.* The hare differs slightly from the rabbit. Hares are born with their eyes open and a full coat of fur. Hares do not have a cotton tail. Hares, rabbits, and pikas are very much alike in their dietary habits.

The Bible uses the Hebrew word *gerah* to describe the hare. This is translated "*cud-chewer*" in most English translations. According to the Talmud, the hare is a ruminant, (Hul. 59a). The Targum defines the cud as something dissolved through rumination, food that becomes pulpy (B. Kam 28b).

The hare does not have the three-or four-chambered stomach which is characteristic of the ruminants. However, it does give its cellulose material a second chewing, and, subsequently, the material goes through a second digestion so that the material missed the first time can be obtained the second time. The stomach of the hare is different from the three- and four-chambered stomachs of cattle, but the function and the end products are essentially the same.

Hares pass two types of fecal material. In addition to the normal waste

179

Photograph courtesy of Amikam Skoob, photographer, Department of Zoology, Tel-Aviv University, Ramat Aviv, Israel.

## The hare

"And the hare, because he cheweth the cud, but divideth not the hoof; he is unclean unto you" (Leviticus 11:6).

material, they pass a second type of pellet known as a caecotroph. The very instant the caecotroph is passed, it is grabbed and chewed again. The caecotrophs are generally passed during late night or very early morning hours, so the average individual may not have observed this process. As soon as the caecotroph is chewed thoroughly and swallowed, it aggregates in the cardiac region of the stomach where it undergoes a second digestion.

Caecotrophs are originally formed in the caecum and are enriched with B vitamins, particularly vitamin $B_1$; they are essential to the hare's diet. The hare not only chews this food again, but the bacterial decomposition of cellulose has the same function as cud-chewing and rumination in paired hoofed animals. It is not an error in the Bible that the hare is classified as a cud-chewer, but a scientific wonder.

Caecotroph formations were first described in the *French Veterinary Journal* in 1882. Since that date, many zoologists have considered this process as rumination. Hares, rabbits, and pikas are designated as ruminants in *Grizimek's Animal Life Encyclopedia,* volume 12, pages 421-422. Dr. Grizimek, chief editor of the encyclopedia, is director of the Frankfort Zoological Gardens in Germany.* The identification of the hare as a ruminant is based primarily on caecotroph formation and bacterial decomposition of cellulose. These are essentially rumination processes.

The hare was forbidden as food in Leviticus 11:6. This restriction was probably because of the presence of blood parasites that can be obtained by handling the carcass. This health rule was very advanced for the time it was given.

---

*Others have noted the similarity to cud-chewing. See Ernest P. Walker, *Mammals of the World*, 2nd ed., vol. 2 (Baltimore: John Hopkins U., 1968), pg. 647.

Photograph courtesy of Amikam Skoob, photographer, Department of Zoology, Tel-Aviv University, Ramat Aviv, Israel.

## The rock hyrax

"The conies [hyraxes] are but a feeble folk, yet make they their houses in the rocks" (Proverbs 30:26).

The dietary regulations given in Leviticus forbid the hyrax as food. The hyrax is now known to consume poisonous plants.

"And the coney [hyrax], because he cheweth the cud, but divideth not the hoof; he is unclean unto you" (Leviticus 11:5).

# 77

# The Hyrax

The Syrian hyrax is the Hebrew *shaphan* of the Bible. It can be identified by the biblical description, as well as from its Arabic name, *tafan*. The Hebrew word *shaphan* is erroneously translated "coney" in Leviticus 11:5, Deuteronomy 14:7, Psalm 104:18, and Proverbs 30:26. The term *coney* is generally applied to the European rabbit. Martin Luther mistakenly translated *shaphan* as "rabbit." This mistake has remained down to the present time in some translations. The scientific name for the hyrax is *Procavia capensis syriaca*.

The hyrax lives in Israel and Jordan along the Arava Valley, the Dead Sea depression, and the Jordan Valley as far north as Upper Galilee. The hyraxes usually live on rocky cliffs. They especially like rock crevices and fissures that open out over a high cliff; this provides protection. Its preference for the rocks is described in Scripture. "The high hills are a refuge for the wild goats; and the rocks for the conies [hyraxes]" (Psalm 104:18).

Hyraxes scamper about the rocks and dangerous cliffs quite easily. The soles of their feet are designed to maintain traction on the rocky ledges. They run and jump with great skill. The forefeet and hind feet have flattened nails resembling hooves, except the second digit of the hind foot. It has a claw used for grooming.

Several females live in a herd with a male. Three or four little ones are born during the spring. The male likes to climb to the highest rocky ledge and sound his territorial call. They scream, chatter, or whistle. They often quarrel among themselves.

The Hebrew word *gerah* is translated as "one that chews the cud." The hyraxes display a frequent chewing motion; they move their jaws sideways like a cud-chewer. The males threaten by exposing their teeth, and this movement looks like a chewing one. These animals resemble the ruminants in many characteristics.

The 1975 *Grzimek's Animal Life Encyclopedia* considers the hyrax as a ruminant. This is based on the fact that the hyrax accomplishes the same thing as a ruminant by means of cellulose digestion. The rumen in cattle is a workshop for bacterial decomposition of cellulose; the hyrax achieves the same thing. The hyrax has a very long protrusion, a caecum, and two additional caeca near the colon. At least one of these protrusions participates in decomposition of cellulose. It contributes certain enzymes necessary for breakdown of the cellulose. It is also believed that the other protrusion, a cone-shaped one, may play some role in metabolizing cellulose. *Grzimek's Animal Life Encyclopedia* states that the hyrax takes care of its cellulose in such a way that the process is considered the same function as rumination in paired-hoofed animals.

*The Handbook of Mammals* (1965) of the Zoological Society of London states that the hyrax has a two-chambered stomach. The stomach of the hyrax is generally considered one-chambered, but it does have a large constriction that gives the stomach the appearance of being two-chambered. Hyraxes have been studied at the Research Zoo of Tel-Aviv University since 1946. These studies have mainly been breeding experiments, and very little data is available on the hyrax's digestive system. A communique from that university indicates they believe the hyrax has a simple stomach. The communique also mentions the very long caecum with the two extra caeca. The *Encyclopedia Judaica* suggests that the complex digestive system of the hyrax is perhaps analogous to the four-chambered stomach of the ruminants.

# 78

# The Camel

The camel of the Bible is the Arabian, or dromedary. This is the one-humped camel whose scientific name is *Camelus dromedarius.* The importance of camels in war is illustrated by the fact they are said to be as numerous as the sands by the sea (Judges 7:12). Camels were an important mode of travel in Abraham's time (Genesis 12:16; 24:11-64). Camels were used to transport goods when the Queen of Sheba came to visit Solomon (1 Kings 10:1-2).

The camel has several mechanisms that help it to survive in the desert. Flexibility of body temperature enables the camel to withstand the extreme desert temperatures. It is able to vary its body temperature several degrees within a day. The ability to utilize nitrogen, concentrate urea, and maintain its blood volume under extremely adverse conditions makes the camel a suitable means of transportation for the desert. A camel can go sometimes as many as four or five days without water. The hump is a fat-storage organ. This keeps the camel supplied with energy long after the food is all consumed. The hump is not a water-storage organ as is often supposed.

Camels are frequently mentioned in the Old Testament. They are a symbol of wealth (Job 42:12) but forbidden to the Jews as meat (Leviticus 11:4). The camel provides milk, transportation, hides and hair for clothing, and dung, which is used as fuel in cooking. The Arabs eat its meat. The hair may be woven into a textured material. This was used for clothing by John the Baptist.

The camels hoof is not divided, but it appears to be divided to the casual observer. Several years ago, Harry Rimmer reported how the atheist Ingersoll denounced the authority of the Scriptures on the basis that he believed Moses had made a mistake. Leviticus 11:4 states, "the camel divideth not the hoof." Ingersoll thought the camel had a divided

Photograph by Harold M. Lambert, Philadelphia, Pa.

A modern camel market at Beer-sheba, similar to those in ancient times.

hoof. It was not Moses who made the mistake but Ingersoll. The camel's foot gives the appearance of being a divided hoof because the toes extend out from pads. The padded feet aid the camel's travel in the desert.

God said unto Moses and Aaron: "Nevertheless these shall ye not eat of them that chew the cud, or of them that divide the hoof: as the camel, because he cheweth the cud, but divideth not the hoof; he is unclean unto you" (Leviticus 11:4).

186

# 79

# The Fiery Serpents

The Hebrew terms, *nachash saraf* in Numbers 21:6, *nachash tsiphoni* in Jeremiah 8:17, Isaiah 59:5, Proverbs 23:32, and *tsepha* of Isaiah 14:29, have been identified by the Jerusalem Biblical Zoo as the Palestinian viper. Its scientific name is *Vipera palestina*. This viper is reported to produce the largest number of snake bites of all venomous snakes in the Holy Land. It is the only deadly snake that goes into the inhabited regions of Israel. It ranges from within the borders of the desert northward. The fiery serpents must have been somewhere in the Negev along the borders of Edom.

The venom of the Palestinian viper is extremely potent and acts on the blood; it is a hematoxin. It produces intense pain, sweating, and vomiting. The affected parts undergo tissue changes and swelling at once. "And the LORD sent fiery serpents [Hebrew *nachash saraf*] . . . and much people of Israel died" (Numbers 21:6). "For behold I will send serpents [*tsiphoni*], cockatrices, [*nachash tsiphoni*] among you, which will not be charmed, and they shall bite you, saith the LORD" (Jeremiah 8:17).

Isaiah 14:29 compares King Hezekiah to the Palestinian viper. Ahaz died, but his son, King Hezekiah, would be an oppressor of the Philistines far worse than his father had been. The verse is used in a comparative sense, but also indicates that as Hezekiah was the offspring of Ahaz, so the fiery flying serpents are the offspring of the Palestinian viper. "Rejoice not, O Philistia, all of you, because the rod [of Judah] that smote thee is broken [Ahaz is dead]; for out of the serpent's root shall come forth an adder [viper] [tsepha meaning King Hezekiah of Judah] and his [the serpent's] offspring will be a fiery flying serpent" (Isaiah 14:29, Amplified Bible).

2 Kings 18 records the action of King Hezekiah against the Philistines. He proved to be a fiery flying serpent. "He [King Hezekiah] smote the

Drawing by Alen Edgar, College Park, Md.

## Palestine viper

For information on poisonous snakes, see *Poisonous Snakes of the World,* Naval Bureau of Medicine and Surgery, 1962.

Philistines, even unto Gaza, and the borders thereof, from the tower of the watchman to the fenced city'' (2 Kings 18:8).

Some snakes give birth to their young alive; others lay eggs. The Palestinian viper is an egg-layer.* The little vipers are extremely mature when the eggs are laid. If the eggs get broken, the young are mature enough to bite. At hatching, most vipers have enough venom to kill at least four mice. Isaiah 59:5 indicates a very accurate observation concerning the Palestinian viper. Note in this verse the crushed eggs break out into a viper. Thus, their maturity is implied. ''They hatch cockatrice' eggs [*tsiphoni* means Palestinian viper] and weave the spider's web: he that eateth their eggs dieth, and that which is crushed breaketh out into a viper'' (Isaiah 59:5).

*Most vipers give birth to their young alive. The Palestinian viper is an exception; it lays eggs. The fact that it is an egg-layer has been verified by the Hebrew University, Israel.

188

The Hebrew word *tsiphoni* is translated *cockatrice* in the King James Version. The cockatrice is a mythological character, and this term should not be used. There is no sound basis for translating *tsiphoni* as *cockatrice*. The verse above is used in a comparative sense, but is also a scientifically accurate description of the viper's eggs.

When the viper bites, it does not hold its victim like some snakes. The viper bites quickly as it pricks the skin with its fangs; they act like a hypodermic needle in delivering the venom. The viper merely needs to cut through the skin; it recoils and strikes again. The entire process is so fast that the human eye can scarcely see what happens. This may perhaps be the meaning of the word *flying*. The word *fiery* most likely comes from the excruciating pain caused by the venom. The pain is accompanied by vomiting and sweating.

The hypodermic technique of delivering its venoh is mentioned in Proverbs 23:32. In this verse, the word translated *stingeth* is the Hebrew word *parash*, literally meaning "to cut into." The verse compares the evils of wine to the bite of the Palestinian viper. The King James Translation is given first, then followed by a rendering of the verse that expresses the idea. "At the last it [wine] biteth like a serpent and stingeth [cuts into] like an adder [Hebrew *tsiphoni* = Palestinian viper]" (Proverbs 23:32). At the last, wine bites like a snake and injects venom like the Palestinian viper.

Drawing by Alen Edgar, College Park, Md.

## The horned sand viper hidden in the path.

Only the outline of the body is seen in the sand; part of its head is sticking out.

# 80

# The Horned Sand Viper

When Jacob gave his dying blessing to the tribes of Israel (Genesis 49), the blessing was prophetic of what would happen to each of the tribes. The tribe of Dan was likened to a serpent, "Dan shall be a serpent by the way, an adder [Hebrew *shefifon*] in the path, that biteth the horse heels, so that his rider shall fall backward" (Genesis 49:17).

The Hebrew *shefifon* refers to the horned sand viper belonging to the genus *Cerastes*. The description of the snake in the path is typical of the practice of this genus. It may be *Cerastes cerastes,* or possibly *Pseudocerastes fieldii.* Horned vipers cover themselves with sand and wait patiently for an opportunity to strike. Only the horns protrude; the outline of the body of the snake can be faintly seen underneath the sand. The viper strikes at the heels of the horses, the tender area above the hooves. Nothing is so subtle as the manner in which the horned viper hides in the sand, then suddenly strikes at a tender spot.

Jacob's blessing to the tribe of Dan is prophetic of the subtle manner in which the tribe would accomplish many things against their enemies. When the serpent suddenly strikes at the heel, the enemy, like the traveler, is unaware of what is happening until it is too late. The tribe of Dan would excell in this subtlety.

Photograph by Amikam Shoob, photographer, Department of Zoology, Tel-Aviv University, Ramat Aviv, Israel.

## The cobra, or asp

Although the species name of the desert cobra, *Walterinnesia aegyptia* means Egyptian, it is commonly called the desert cobra to distinguish it from the Egyptian cobra known as *Naja haje*. The black, glossy scales of the desert cobra distinguish it from the Egyptian cobra, which is rather dull. *Walterinnesia aegyptia* is distributed throughout most of the nations of the Middle East.

The desert cobra will not rear up or hood like the Egyptian or Indian cobra; therefore, it is said not to be charmed or enchanted. "Surely the serpent will bite without enchantment; and a babbler is no better" (Ecclesiastes 10:11).

# 81

# The Cobra, or Asp

The Hebrew word *pethen* is a term applied to the cobra. It is translated four times as "asp" and two times as "adder" in the King James Version. Most books and commentaries suggest that the cobra of the Bible is the Egyptian cobra, *Naja haje*. This seems impossible in view of the following information. First, the Egyptian cobra does not live in Israel, and only solitary specimens have been reported to exist in the Negev and Sinai. Second, the cobra of the Bible is said to be one that cannot be charmed (Psalm 58:4-5). The Egyptian cobra can be charmed; thus, it is eliminated as a possibility. The desert cobra of Israel cannot be charmed and is probably the Hebrew *pethen* of the Scriptures. The scientific name of the desert cobra is *Walterinnesia aegyptia*.

The desert cobra is a very large, black snake. Its venom acts on the nervous system to produce paralysis; it is a neurotoxin. According to the handbooks of toxicology, there is no antivenin for this cobra. Its venom is about as strong as the Indian cobra's. Fortunately this species is not very abundant at the present time.

One of the most unusual passages concerning the cobra is in the book of Isaiah. Chapter 11 describes the peacefulness of the kingdom when the animals will no longer devour one another. Their carnivorous eating habits will be changed; they will be herbivorous. It is within this same context of the kingdom that a description of the cobra and viper are given. The words *asp* and *cockatrice* are changed to *cobra* and *viper,* according to their Hebrew meanings. "And the sucking child shall play on the hole of the asp [desert cobra], and the weaned child shall put his hand on the cockatrice' [Palestinian viper's] den" (Isaiah 11:8).

# 82

# The Deaf Adder

Perhaps nothing has caused so much controversy among biologists as the hearing mechanism of snakes. Snakes do not have an external ear, a middle ear, or an eardrum. They are deaf to airborne sounds but sensitive to vibrations. The ear bone of the snake is attached to the bone supporting the lower jawbone. This picks up vibrations from the ground or substratum on which the snake is resting. The tongue has also been reported to be sensitive to vibrations. Psalm 58:4-5 reveals a truth that man has had great difficulty in determining. "Their poison is like the poison of a serpent: they are like the deaf adder [cobra] that stoppeth her ear; which will not hearken to the voice of charmers, charming never so wisely."

The word *adder* is a translation of the Hebrew *pethen*; this is the asp, or cobra. The asp of the Old Testament is the equivalent of the Greek *aspis* of the New Testament (Romans 3:13).

Since snakes are deaf to sounds in the air, the cobra does not hear the sound of the gourd flute played by the charmer. An alarmed cobra holds its body erect when it is frightened. The noise of the gourd flute has no effect; the snake reacts to the movements of the charmer.

A scientific observation is in Psalm 58:5; it states that the cobra charms "never so wisely." The Egyptian and Indian cobra can be charmed, but the desert cobra of Israel cannot be charmed. Furthermore, Psalm 58:5 indicates that the cobra is deaf to airborne sounds, "which will not hearken to the voice of charmers, charming never so wisely."

# 83

# The Serpent's Tongue

Verses mentioning the snake's tongues are constantly under attack. Such verses are usually said to contain an error or a myth. Careful analysis of these verses will reveal they contain a highly scientific truth. The verses most frequently criticized are:

He shall suck the poison of asps [cobras]: the viper's tongue shall slay him (Job 20:16).

They [evil men] have sharpened their tongues like a serpent; adders' poison is under their lips (Psalm 140:3).

Their throat is an open sepulchre; with their tongues they have used deceit; the poison of asps [cobras] is under their lips (Romans 3:13).

These verses are cited in various references as being a misunderstanding of the Hebrews or a myth. Job 20:16 does not say the tongue delivers the poison, but it does imply that the tongue is involved in the slaying. Psalm 140:3 and Romans 3:13 clearly and correctly state where the venom is located.

Snake venom is a special type of saliva produced in glands that are comparable to the salivary glands; venom is like poisonous saliva. The venom glands are located under the lips, usually in the very back part of the mouth. In a few species, the glands are under the lips, near the eye regions. Some snakes spit their venom instead of injecting it; this type of venom can cause the loss of an eye. There has been some question about the translation of Psalm 140:3. In order to give additional proof of the location of the venom, Romans 3:13 is also quoted.

All snakes have a forked tongue that is long and sharp-pointed. When the tongue is not in use, it is drawn into a tubular sheath in the lower part of the mouth. The snake's tongue constantly licks the dust in order to keep the snake informed of its environment. Tasting the dust tells the snake if a lizard or a mouse is available for dinner. This method of sampling the dust is mentioned in Micah 7:17, "They shall lick the dust like a serpent." This method of analysis of air molecules and dust is called *chemoreception.* In the roof of the snake's mouth is a smelling structure called the Jacobson's organ. The tongue carries the molecules or particles to the Jacobson's organ for analysis. Tests show that some snakes can track a rabbit that has already been carefully buried several miles away. Some snakes threaten or intimidate their prey with their tongues. This method is often used to catch birds. The tongue is sensitive to almost anything in the environment, including vibrations.

Only recently have scientists undertaken tests to determine the sensitivity of the Jacobson's organ. Yet God said they used their tongues to lick. Man completely ignored this statement or criticized it as an error.

Job 20:16 states that the viper's tongue shall slay the wicked. This makes reference to the manner in which the snake's tongue keenly sets up its prey. It implies that what the wicked sucked so sweetly will prove to be the poison of asps [cobras]. In Job 20:15 he swallowed the riches but they turn bitter and he will vomit them.

The sharpened tongue refers to the sharp forked tongue of the snake (Romans 3:13). The snake's tongue is used to catch its prey. So it is with a person who speaks with a forked tongue, full of lies and deceit. The snake's tongue is harmless, but it helps the snake in the deadly strike.

A similar illustration is found in Psalm 5:9: "For there is no faithfulness in their mouth; their inward part is very wickedness; their throat is an open sepulchre; they flatter with their tongue".

The flattering tongue of a fast talker is like a viper's tongue setting up its victim. Most of the previous verses are comparing things; nevertheless, the verses contain a scientific truth, for it is the tongue of the snake that samples the air and dust and sets the snake in readiness for the strike.

The use of *sharp-pointed* in describing the snake's tongue does not mean that the tongue is hard or piercing; the tongue is extremely flexible. *Sharp-pointed* refers to the shape; it ends in two fine points. These two fine points of the tongue convey particles to the Jacobson's organ for chemical analysis.

Photograph by Amikam Shoob, photographer, Department of Zoology, Tel-Aviv University, Ramat Aviv, Israel.

## *Echis colorata*

*Echis* is an extremely aggressive, venomous snake that will bite anything that disturbs it. The Echis moves by throwing loops over itself in movements similar to those of the sidewinder. These characteristics have caused some writers to consider it as the fiery flying serpent. Both Echis and the fiery flying serpent come from the desert regions: "The burden of the beasts of the south: into the land of trouble and anguish, from whence come the young and old lion, the viper [*epheh*] and fiery flying serpent" (Isaiah 30:6).

# 84

# The Saw-scaled Viper

The Hebrew word *epheh* is generally translated "adder" in the King James Version. All the words in Scripture pertaining to snakes have been rather indiscriminately translated. The same Hebrew word is sometimes translated "viper" in one verse and "cobra" in another. The English word *adder* means "viper." Adder is derived from the Old English *naedra*. *Naedra* was eventually changed to *nadder*, then the initial letter was dropped forming the word *adder*. *Adder* is equivalent to the Latin *vipera* from which we derive our English word *viper*. The word *viper* may be used to denote a venomous snake, or it may be used to mean a certain type of snake. The reason it is used in a general sense to mean venomous snake probably is that vipers are among the most venomous snakes, particularly the pit vipers.

The Hebrew word *epheh* refers to a venomous snake of the desert regions of Israel. It is generally translated "viper" in the Scriptures. In other Jewish writings, the Midrash mentions a snake called *ekhes*. This seems to be the genus *Echis*. *Echis* also fits the Hebrew word meaning "to cry." When *Echis* is angry or frightened, it coils into a figure eight then makes a noise by rubbing its saw-toothed scales together. This makes a sharp crying sound. The expanded body of the snake acts like a sounding board and amplifies the noise.

There are two species of *Echis* in the desert areas of Israel: *Echis colorata* and *Echis carinatus*. The biblical *epheh* could be either species, but it is most likely *Echis colorata* because of its distribution in this area. The two species are much alike except *colorata* is more colorful.

198

# VII

# BOTANY AND MICROBIOLOGY

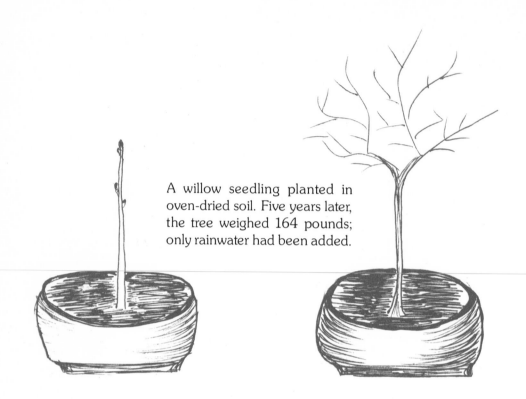

A willow seedling planted in oven-dried soil. Five years later, the tree weighed 164 pounds; only rainwater had been added.

## Plant growth and development

Above is the scheme of the experiment conducted by Jan Baptista van Helmont which demonstrated that a large portion of the nourishment came from rainwater. Prior to this, Aristotle had proposed that plants obtain all their nourishment from soil by means of preformed particles that were absorbed without important chemical changes.

The conclusions of van Helmont were partially wrong, mainly because the chemistry of photosynthesis was not known at that time. His contributions to plant physiology were important because he showed that water is necessary for plant growth and development. The major part of the weight of the plant consists of water; the dry weight of a plant constitutes a smaller portion of the total weight.

# 85

# Plant Growth and Development

The green plant uses water, carbon dioxide, and the sun's energy to manufacture sugar. This complicated chemical process is known as photosynthesis. Step by step, scientists have been able to unravel the complexities of this process. As we review these experiments, keep in mind that the Bible mentions the role of water and sunlight in plant growth and development.

Jan Baptista van Helmont (1577-1640), a Belgian chemist and physician, was the first to produce experimental evidence that water constituted a large portion of plant growth. He planted a willow seedling in oven-dried soil. At the beginning of the experiment, the soil weighed 200 pounds. He weighed the willow seedling, then planted it in the oven-dried soil. During the next five years he watered the seedling with only rainwater.

At the end of the five-year experiment, the seedling had grown to 164 pounds. The soil in which the willow was grown was oven-dried and weighed again. The soil had lost only a few ounces of its initial weight. He concluded that the bulk of plant nourishment comes from rainwater.

Hundreds, even thousands of years before van Helmont's experiment, God indicated that rain served as the nourishment for a tree: "He planteth an ash, and the rain doth nourish it" (Isaiah 44: 14b).

# 86

# The Role of Sunshine in Plant Growth and Development

In 1804, Theodore de Saussure published experiments that demonstrated the carbon of plants came from carbon dioxide. He was not sure if sunlight was required, although he was unable to get photosynthesis without it. The German scientist, Julius Mayer (1844), concluded that the metabolic energy of plants was derived from the sun's energy by means of photosynthesis. His conclusions were based on experimental data obtained from the energy released by burning plants.

Today scientists recognize that, in addition to photosynthesis, sunshine affects flowering and fruit production in plants. These experiments are especially interesting, in view of the mention of sunlight in the Bible in relation to fruit production.

And this is the blessing, wherewith Moses the man of God blessed the children of Israel before his death. . . . And of Joseph he said, Blessed of the LORD be his land, for the precious things of heaven, for the dew, and for the deep that coucheth beneath, . . . And for the precious fruits brought forth by the sun (Deuteronomy 33:1, 13, 14a).

It is obvious that God is in complete control of plant growth and development. God allows the physical laws of nature to take effect, but He is ultimately in control of all of these laws: "He causeth the grass to grow for the cattle, and herb for the service of man: that he may bring forth food out of the earth" (Psalm 104:14). "Sing unto the LORD with thanksgiving . . . who covereth the heaven with clouds, who prepareth rain for the earth, who maketh grass to grow upon the mountains" (Psalm 147:7a, 8).

# 87

# Grafting

Grafting is an ancient horticultural process. A cutting from a good plant is attached to the rooted stem of a hardy or wild stock. The rooted stem on which the graft is placed is called the *rootstock*. The cutting is called a *scion* (or cion). Grafting is done in a variety of ways; cleft grafting, whip grafting or budding. This is done mainly because the rootstock is undesirable for fruit production, but may have great resistance to disease and insects.

In a graft, the growing regions of the cutting and rootstock must be placed together so the cambial layers, containing the growth cells, will make contact. The growth cells must be in close contact in order for the graft to take.

The apostle Paul uses the illustration of grafting in Romans 11, and there are many comparisons we might make from this horticultural technique. In Romans 11:24, we learn that God grafts contrary to nature. The gentiles, the wild stock, represent the scion. The Jews represent the natural rootstock. This graft is the reverse of the horticultural technique. The gentiles should not boast of their position for it is the rootstock that supports the graft of the wild branches. Furthermore, there is a horticultural aspect illustrated here; the original branches, the Jews, are more closely related to their own rootstock and would be easy to graft back again.

The Jews must have understood this illustration of grafting. The olive tree grows wild in the Orient and is grafted; this greatly facilitates fruit production. Paul reminds the Jews once again in Romans 11:23 that God is able to graft them in again.

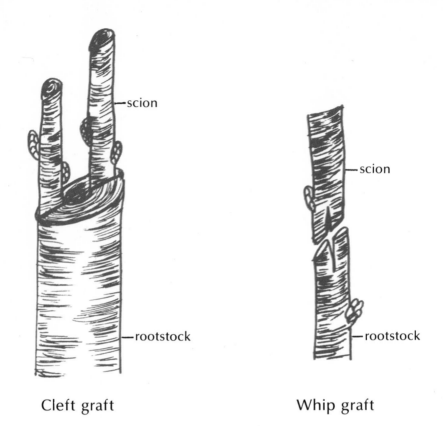

Cleft graft                    Whip graft

"For if thou wert cut out of the olive tree which is wild by nature, and wert graffed contrary to nature into a good olive tree: how much more shall these, which be the natural branches, be graffed into their own olive tree?" (Romans 11:24).

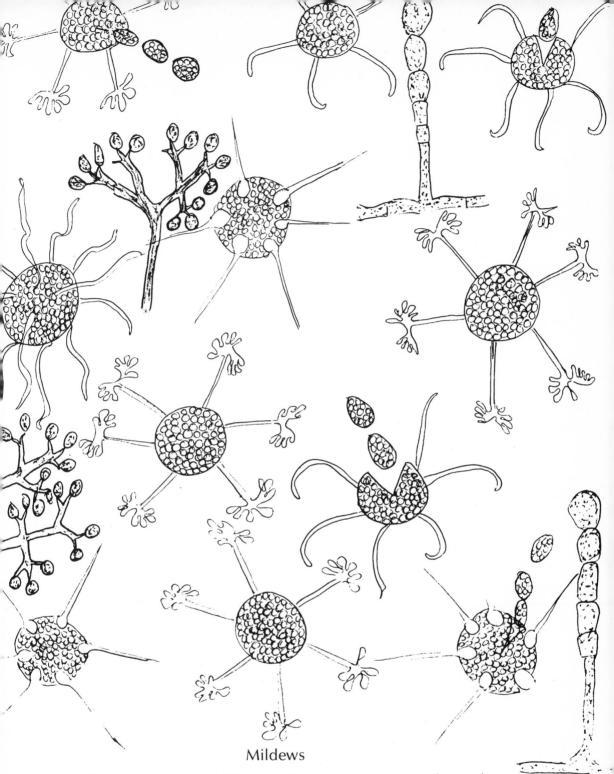

## Mildews

"I have smitten you with blasting and mildew: when your gardens and your vineyards and your fig trees and your olive trees increased, the palmerworm devoured them: yet have ye not returned unto me, saith the LORD" (Amos 4:9).

205

# 88

# Mildew and Blight

Mildew and blight are fungus diseases. In Scripture, the blight and mildew are said to infect gardens, vineyards, fig trees, and olive trees as a chastening from the Lord. The two groups of mildews that cause serious diseases of plants are the downy and the powdery mildews.

Downy mildews are obligate parasites that cause serious diseases on cultivated plants such as onions, lettuce, grapes, cucurbits, beans, peas, and various grasses. The powdery mildews are also serious pests that attack apples, grapes, clover, grasses, peas, and beans. Some attack only one plant. Others will attack a wide variety of plants. The reference to mildews is to a group of diseases rather than to a specific genera, or species. Some fungi that fit the description given in the Bible may be relatively new to an area. Therefore, it is difficult to equate present-day pests with those in ancient times.

The term blight (blasting) is a general term used to designate the fungus diseases known as smuts and rusts. These destroy thousands of dollars worth of grain each year. The most familiar are wheat rust and corn smut. The reference to smuts and rusts in the Bible covers a whole host of plant pathogens. There are approximately 4,000 kinds of rusts and at least 900 or more smuts. Rusts attack rye, oats, pears, plums, fig trees, and numerous other plants. Smuts attack barley, oats, rye, and various grains.

God's hand is seen in complete control of the environment, even the diseases of plants.

Photograph of the cedars of Lebanon by Harold M. Lambert, Philadelphia, Pa.

"And he [Solomon] spake of trees, from the cedar tree that is in Lebanon even unto the hyssop that springeth out of the wall: he spake also of beasts, and of fowl, and of creeping things, and of fishes" (1 Kings 4:33).

Photograph courtesy of Rev. Richard Knox, missionary in the Middle East, United Missionary Fellowship.

## The role of sunshine in plant growth and development

A typical Middle East fruit market exhibits the precious fruits brought forth by the sun.

Precious fruits are brought forth by the sun just as God said in Deuteronomy 33:14. This biblical statement was made thousands of years before man knew the role of sunshine in plant growth and development.

# 89

# Red Fretting Leprosy

"And if the plague be greenish or reddish in the garment, or in the skin [leather], either in the warp, or in the woof, or in anything of skin; it is a plague of leprosy, and shall be shewed unto the priest: and the priest shall look upon the plague, and shut it that hath the plague seven days: and he shall look on the plague on the seventh day; if the plague be spread in the garment, either in the warp, or in the woof, or in a skin, or in any work that is made of skin; the plague is a fretting leprosy; it is unclean" (Leviticus 13:49-51).

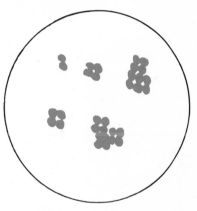

Drawing of red bacteria commonly found on red-spotted leather hides.

The ancient Egyptians and Hebrews tanned leather by first soaking the skin in a solution of lime water to remove the hair. The skin was then placed in a solution of oak bark and water. The oak provided the tannins, a source of tannic acid. Although the lime solution has been used for years, it was recently discovered that the hairs are removed by bacterial action on the skins. The bacteria that remove the hairs normally occur in the lime solution. The solution may also contain certain undesirable contaminants which cause fretting or weakening of skins. Bacterial attack on hides is known today as "red heat." It is responsible for great losses to the leather industry, chiefly by red spotting and weakening of leather fibers. Losses have been reported by major hide-producing countries of the world.

The weakening of pelts due to red heat is not limited to one type of bacteria; several genera have been reported to cause spotting. Several types of bacteria have been isolated from damaged hides secured from tanneries located in various parts of the world. The red fretting leprosy in garments may have been organisms such as those known today to cause red heat.

# 90

# Green Fretting Leprosy

"And if the plague be greenish" (Leviticus 13:49a).

To the left is a drawing of the green mold, *aspergillus*, which is a frequent contaminant of cloth and leather.

The green molds of aspergillus are distributed throughout the world. They normally grow in the soil, and their spores are blown about with the dust. Several species of this mold grow on cloth and leather. They discolor fabrics, cause a musty odor, and damage the fibers.

Many organisms are beneficial because they are utilized in the retting of flax and hemp, but a large number of these are undesirable and cause great losses to the textile industry. Various ones attack silk, wool, linen, and cotton. Of all the organisms that attack textiles, aspergillus is probably the most troublesome.

It seems likely that the green fretting leprosy of the Bible was one of the green molds of aspergillus, especially since it is such a nuisance on leather and fabrics of all types. Most leather hides are cured today by means of a brine solution followed by an inhibitor of mold and bacteria; nevertheless, contamination still occurs.

The fungus *chaetomium* frequently accompanies the aspergilli in their attack on cellulose fibers. These may have been present along with the aspergilli. Both organisms occur in soil, dust, straw, and various other materials. They grow abundantly in a warm, humid climate.

# 91

# The Red and Green
# Leprosy in Houses

It is a popular belief that the fretting leprosy of houses was a lichen. The red contaminant in houses could have been a lichen, but this is extremely doubtful. Lichens have two components; they are part alga and part fungus. The algal component requires sunshine for photosynthesis. They grow well in subdued sunlight but won't grow without at least some sunshine. Lichens are extremely sensitive to any type of pollution, particularly smoke. It is difficult to get them to grow where there are fires, cooking fumes, or other contaminating things. They grow well outside on old roofs made of wooden shingles or on rocks and bricks. They are not found indoors, because the algal component requires sunshine. Even under ideal conditions they grow very slowly, and rarely could they be considered a nuisance.

Lichens are not harmful. According to Leviticus, the red and green leprosy appear to be harmful; they are a contaminant in the mortar and stones. "And he shall cause the house to be scraped within round about, and they shall pour out the dust that they scrape off without the city into an unclean place: and they shall take other stones, and put them in the place of those stones; and he shall take other mortar, and shall plaister the house" (Leviticus 14:41-42).

The red contaminant of houses was probably the various bacteria that grow abundantly in plaster of certain types. There are several kinds of bacteria that contaminate plaster, depending on the ingredients used in the plaster mixture. Some of these bacteria would be far more destructive than lichens.

Several kinds of mortar were used by the Israelites. Mud and clay were often mixed with chopped straw. A cement compound of lime, ashes, and sand was also used. The nature of these substances made them suscepti-ble to bacterial attack. It seems that the red fretting leprosy of houses would be bacteria rather than other types of contaminants. The bacteria would be a natural contaminant of the ingredients of the mortar.

Some have suggested that red fungi instead of red bacteria was the red fretting leprosy. This does not seem likely. Fungi grow well in darkness inside a house (not those of the lichen association). Although fungi will grow abundantly without sunlight, there are practically no red ones that would be associated with attack on plaster or mortar.

The green fretting leprosy of houses is most likely various species of the fungus aspergillus. The aspergilli cause several diseases. Some produce a toxic substance that causes cancer. Still others cause aspergillosis, a lung disease that closely resembles tuberculosis.

Both bacteria and aspergillus fungus can cause disease in persons. According to Leviticus 14:47, the green fretting leprosy and the red fretting leprosy were considered harmful to people. "And he that lieth in the house shall wash his clothes; and he that eateth in the house shall wash his clothes" (Leviticus 14:47).

# 92

# Fuller's Soap

Fuller's soap was a type of alkaline solution used for cleaning garments (Jeremiah 2:22, Malachi 3:2). It had a bleaching effect. At the transfiguration of our Lord his garments became white as no fuller's soap can get them, "And after six days Jesus taketh with him Peter, and James, and John, and leadeth them up into a high mountain apart by themselves: and he was transfigured before them. And his raiment became shining, exceedingly white as snow; so as no fuller on earth can white them" (Mark 9:2-3).

The cleaning solution mentioned in Jeremiah 2:22 is the Hebrew word *nether,* which is translated "nitre" in the King James Version. Nitre is potassium nitrate. The use of the word *nitre* does not convey the true meaning of the Hebrew, because nitre has no cleaning properties. The same word appears in Proverbs 25:20 where it reacts with vinegar (acetic acid). This chemical reaction with vinegar and potassium or sodium carbonate is possible, but not with nitre. The Hebrew word *nether* probably means natron, or sodium carbonate. Natron was mined in Egypt and used on mummies. The Israelites would have known of this chemical, but it is doubtful that the pure chemical was used in fullering, because the Talmud specifies plant ashes as the source for the fuller's soap.

The reference to fuller's soap most likely refers to ashes of plants. Some plants accumulate both potassium and sodium salts; others accumulate only one or the other. Plants that grow in salt marshes can accumulate enough salt to be used as a salt substitute. According to the Talmud, *borith* was a perennial plant used for cleaning. The Hebrew words *bor* and *borith* are used in reference to cleanliness and soap. In ancient times, salts were derived from plants that belong to the following genera: *Salicornia, Atriplex, Salsola, Saponaria,* and *Statice.* Several species of *Salsola* (prickley saltwort) are found in the Negev.

213

The fuller was the person who cleaned clothes, and, in all probability, he trampled the clothing to wash it. This is indicated by the derivation of the word *wash* in Exodus 19:10 and 2 Samuel 19:24. The Hebrew word is kabas, which is derived from *kabash*, meaning "to tread." A fuller's field with a highway that passed through it was located very close to the city wall of Jerusalem (2 Kings 18:17; Isaiah 7:1-3).

The chemical process of modern day soap making is called saponification. This process was not known in ancient times; it appears somewhat later. Saponification is the heating of a fatty substance with an alkali to produce fatty acid salts. Fatty acid salts constitute soap as we know it today. If olive oil is used as the fatty component, the soap is called castile. The Middle East is noted for the castile soap made at Neapolis.

The accompanying drawings are of salt marsh plants probably used by the fuller in ancient times.

God said "For though thou wash thee with nitre, and take thee much soap, yet thine iniquity is marked before me, saith the Lord GOD" (Jeremiah 2:22). "But who may abide the day of his coming? And who shall stand when he appeareth? For he is like a refiner's fire, and like fullers' soap" (Malachi 3:2).

Salsola        Atriplex

214

# VIII

# ANATOMY AND
# PHYSIOLOGY

"The hearing ear, and                    "the seeing eye,

the LORD hath made even both of them" (Proverbs 20:12).

# 93

# The Eye

David prayed, "Keep me as the apple of the eye, hide me under the shadow of thy wings" (Psalm 17:8).

The pupil of the eye is mentioned in Scripture under the Hebrew word *babah,* meaning "gate," or "opening" (Zechariah 2:8). It is unique that the Hebrew lanaguage is scientifically correct when it calls the pupil a gate, or opening. The pupil is the opening in the eye that allows light to enter. The muscular adjustments of the eye open and close the pupil, to allow enough light for good vision.

Drawing by Alen Edgar, College Park, Md.

The pupil of the eye is also referred to by the Hebrew word *ishon,* which literally means "little man" (Psalm 17:8). This "little man" refers to the miniature image seen in the pupil. If you will stand in subdued light and look into another person's eye, you will see the reflection of this "little man."

In reference to the nation of Israel, the Hebrew word *bath* is used as an affectionate statement concerning God's love for the nation of Israel. She is called the daughter of the eye. Israel was a very precious aperture through which the Messiah was revealed. "For he that toucheth you toucheth the apple of his eye" (Zechariah 2:8b). "Let not the apple of thine eye cease" (Lamentations 2:18b).

According to Scripture, the eyes of the Lord are constantly watching the nation of Israel; she is truly the apple of his eye. "A land which the LORD thy God careth for: the eyes of the LORD thy God are always upon it, from the beginning of the year even unto the end of the year" (Deuteronomy 11:12).

217

# 94

# The Heart and the Blood

William Harvey (1628), an English physician and medical college lecturer, proved that the blood circulates from the heart through the arteries and back to the heart through the veins. Harvey knew there were small vessels that united the veins and arteries, but he was unable to prove it. Shortly after Harvey's death, an Italian doctor, Marcello Malpighi, discovered these vessels. He called them *capillaries.*

The ancient Egyptians thought blood moved back and forth through channels; they did not understand its circular pathway. They thought the blood contained urine and tears. The Greeks contributed very little to this field of study. Galen thought the blood contained spirits and that twenty-seven pulses existed. Thousands of years prior to the work of Harvey, the Scripture suggested the function of the heart in supplying the flesh with this life-giving substance. "A sound heart is the life of the flesh" (Proverbs 14:30). The Scripture further indicates that this life-giving substance moves through the flesh, thus it implies circulation. "For the life of the flesh is in the blood" (Leviticus 17:11).

When bone cells mature, they become calcified and no longer are able to communicate with the blood and tissue fluids. Living bone cells, particularly the growing regions of the bone, must continually communicate with the blood and tissue fluids. The function of the marrow and the bathing of the tissue fluids is seen in Job 21:24, "His bones are moistened with marrow." The following verse implies a fine differentiation between the bone cells and the marrow. "The word of God is quick, and powerful, and sharper than any twoedged sword, piercing even to the dividing asunder of soul and spirit, and of the joints and marrow, and is a discerner of the thoughts and intents of the heart" (Hebrews 4:12).

One of the most frequent references to blood is the passover lamb, which foreshadows the Messiah in every detail. The blood of the lamb was to be placed on the two side posts and on the upper doorposts of the house, forming a cross. Note carefully that it was not to be placed on the doorstep, because it was not to be trodden under foot. This passover lamb depicted the true Lamb of God. Abraham foresaw this Lamb when he said, "God will provide himself a lamb" (Genesis 22:8).

The Messiah, the Lamb of God, would be the one who would fulfill all of God's and man's requirements. The Messiah would be the one who could stand in the gap, "And I sought for a man among them, that should make up the hedge, and stand in the gap" (Ezekiel 22:30). The Messiah would fulfill the requirements of the daysman, "Neither is there any daysman betwixt us, that might lay his hand upon us both" (Job 9:33). The Messiah would also be the one who could stand in the breach as typified by Moses, "Therefore he said that he would destroy them, had not Moses his chosen stood before him in the breach" (Psalm 106:23). In the New Testament, Christ is the mediator. "For there is one God, and one mediator between God and men, the man Christ Jesus" (1 Timothy 2:5).

### The blood of the lamb foreshadows the cross

"And they shall take of the blood, and strike it on the two side posts and on the upper doorpost of the houses.... And the blood shall be to you for a token upon the houses where ye are: and when I see the blood, I will pass over you, and the plague shall not be upon you to destroy you, when I smite the land of Egypt" (Exodus 12:7, 13).

Photograph by Harold M. Lambert, Philadelphia, Pa.

219

# 95

# Embryonic Development

Part of Psalm 139 gives a beautiful description of the embryonic development of an individual. It implies the uniting of the cells, which is translated as *knit* in the King James Version. It also describes the skeletal framework by the use of the Hebrew word *etsem*, which means literally, "bone." This psalm gives God's divine blueprint for each person. Not only does God foresee every minute detail of each individual's development, but He sees all the days of his life before he is born; this is mentioned in verse 16. A literal translation of Psalm 139 follows with an explanation of verses 13-17.

13. "For thou didst form my internal organs: Thou didst knit me" unite my cells "together in my mother's uterus." The Hebrew word *kelayoth* literally means *kidneys*, but it is used to imply the internal organs.

14. "I will praise thee for I am fearfully and wonderfully made: Marvelous are thy works; and of this my soul is well aware." A person is fearfully made because he is so frail and weak; he is wonderfully made because of all the intricate parts.

15. "My skeletal framework was not hidden from thee when I was made in secret and intricately wrought in the lowest parts of the earth." "My skeletal framework" comes from the Hebrew word *etsem*, which means bone. The phrase, "Lowest parts of the earth," as in the King James Version, is poetical for lowest parts of the abdomen, or uterus.)

16. "Your eyes have seen my embryo and in thy book all of my parts were recorded. All the days of my life were accounted for when as yet there were none of them." The Hebrew word *golem* is translated *substance* in the King James Version. *Golem* means either fetus or embryo.

220

17. "How precious also are thy thoughts unto me, O God: How great is the sum of them."

The complexity of embryonic development is further seen in Ecclesiastes 11:5, where bone development in the uterus is compared with the complexity of the work of the Holy Spirit, "As thou knowest not what is the way of the spirit, nor how the bones do grow in the womb of her that is with child."

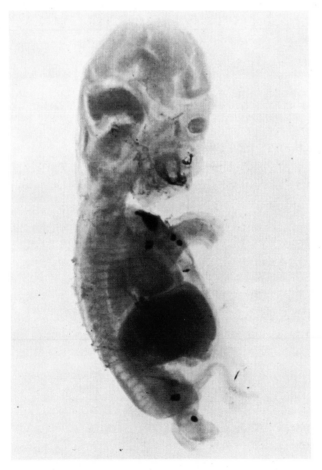

Photograph courtesy of Carolina Biological Supply Co., Burlington, N.C.

## A twenty-two millimeter human embryo approximately 7½ to 8 weeks old.

"I will praise thee; for I am fearfully and wonderfully made" (Psalm 139:14).

# 96

# Life Expectancy

A marvelous scientific statement is in Psalm 90:10. This verse indicates that seventy years is about as long as we can expect to live. A score is twenty years, and 3 score is sixty, plus ten years equals seventy. If you are especially strong, you might live four score, which is four times twenty years, or a total of eighty years.

The life expectancy chart below merely illustrates the truth of Scripture. Some nations fall short of this expectancy because of extremely high disease rates and starvation.

LIFE EXPECTANCY*

| Country | Years | Country | Years |
|---|---|---|---|
| Norway | 73 years | Scotland | 69 |
| Sweden | 73 | Germany | 69 |
| Netherlands | 72 | U.S.S.R. | 68 |
| Israel | 72 | Japan | 67 |
| New Zealand | 71 | Argentina | 60 |
| Denmark | 71 | Ceylon | 60 |
| England | 71 | Brazil | 53 |
| Wales | 71 | Chile | 52 |
| France | 70 | Mexico | 51 |
| Australia | 70 | Cambodia | 43 |
| Czechoslovakia | 70 | India | 32 |
| United States | 70 | Central Republic of Africa | 32 |

"The days of our years are threescore years and ten; and if by reason of strength they be fourscore years. . . . So teach us to number our days, that we may apply our hearts unto wisdom" (Psalm 90:10, 12).

*Data from 1961 *United Nations Yearbook*

# 97

# Dust Thou Art

It wasn't until the late eighteenth and the early ninteenth centuries that man developed chemical techniques sufficiently accurate for analysis of protoplasm and mineral residues. Chemical analysis of the mineral residue of man shows that he is made of the same materials as the dust of the earth. A 155-pound man used to be worth approximately $1.98 in mineral residue, but with current inflation he is worth about $4.98. Below is the mineral analysis of a 155-pound man. The mineral content reveals he is dust, just as the Scripture described him thousands of years ago.

"Like as a father pitieth his children, so the LORD pitieth them that fear him. For he knoweth our frame; he remembereth that we are dust" (Psalm 103:13-14).

| calcium | 43.5% | sulfur | 7.1 |
|---|---|---|---|
| chlorine | 4.3 | magnesium | 1.4 |
| sodium | 4.3 | phosphorus | 29.1 |
| potassium | 10.2 | iron | .1 |

plus traces of iodine, manganese, silicon, copper, and other minerals.

According to Scripture, man is made of dust of the earth. "For dust thou art, and dust shalt thou return" (Genesis 3:19b). God has so wonderfully provided nature with minute undertakers, whose job it is to bring about the degradation process. "The worm shall feed sweetly on him" (Job 24:20). Through the degradation process, the dust is returned to the earth then the spirit to the Lord: "Then shall the dust return to the earth as it was: and the spirit return unto God who gave it" (Ecclesiastes 12:7). The apostle Paul describes death as being "absent from the body . . . present with the Lord" (2 Corinthians 5:8b).

The scientific accuracy of the Scripture is verified by such statements, especially since these statements were made thousands of years before man developed chemical techniques for such analyses.

# 98

# The Breath of Life

Respiration is the basic metabolic process of human life. Cells need a continuous supply of oxygen, which is brought to them by the red blood cells via the lungs. Some living things are capable of obtaining oxygen directly from compounds, instead of using atmospheric oxygen. Human blood contains a protein known as hemoglobin which combines with oxygen to form oxyhemoglobin. It is oxyhemoglobin that makes the cheeks and lips rosy. When cells use the oxygen, the hemoglobin is said to be reduced. Reduced hemoglobin is blue and imparts this color to the tissues. When circulation is impaired or death occurs, the blue color appears.

The importance of breath may be best illustrated by a drowning person. When a person is near drowning and there is no apparent breath, there may be sufficient oxygen for the cells to carry on their life functions, so that resuscitation causes the breathing process to continue. In the case of Lazarus, more than restoration of breath was required because decomposition had set in (John 11:39).

There has been a great deal of discussion about euthanasia. At what point does death occur? The biological definitions of life and death are sometimes philosophical in nature. In general, life is defined by a list of characteristics such as the ability to reproduce, respiration, and movement. A person must possess some of these, but not all, to be considered alive. Death is defined as the cessation of life processes, or the absence of life.

Scripture speaks of "the breath of life," and indicates that death is a withdrawal of the God-given breath. Since oxygen is essential to human life, the Scriptural definition of life and death appears more logical and scientific than some found in textbooks. Life is defined in Scripture in terms of breath: "And breathed into his nostrils the breath of life" (Genesis 2:7). Death is defined as the withdrawal of the God-given breath. "Thou takest away their breath, they die, and return to their dust" (Psalm 104:29).

Photograph by Harold M. Lambert, Philadelphia, Pa.

The bulging throat of a singing toad.

"Let everything that hath breath praise the LORD" (Psalm 150:6).
"In whose hand is the soul of every living thing, and the breath of all mankind" (Job 12:10).

# 99

# The Aging Process

In Ecclesiastes 12, Solomon admonishes the adolescent to remember his Creator before old age occurs. Solomon's admonition is followed by a detailed description of the aging process. He wants to impress upon the adolescent that it is too late to serve the Lord after old age and senility have arrived.

1. Remember now thy Creator in the days of thy youth, while the evil days come not, nor the years draw nigh, when thou shalt say, I have no pleasure in them;

2. While the sun, or the light, or the moon, or the stars, be not darkened, nor the clouds return after the rain:

3. In the day when the keepers of the house shall tremble, and the strong men shall bow themselves, and the grinders cease because they are few, and those that look out of the windows be darkened,

4. And the doors shall be shut in the streets, when the sound of the grinding is low, and his voice shall become as that of a bird, and all the daughters of music shall be brought low;

5. Yea, they shall be afraid of high places, and terrors shall be for them even on level, and the almond tree shall flourish, and the grasshopper shall be a burden, and the caper-berry shall fail; because man goeth to his long home, and the mourners go about the streets:

6. Or ever the silver cord be loosed, or the golden bowl be broken, or the pitcher be broken at the fountain, or the wheel broken at the cistern.

7. And the dust return to the earth as it was: and the spirit return unto God who gave it.

8. Vanity of vanities, saith the preacher; all is vanity (Ecclesiastes 12:1-8).*

---

*Ecclesiastes 12:1-8 quoted by permission from *The Pentateuch with Haftaroth and Five Megiloth,* a revision by Alexander Harkavy, published by the Hebrew Publishing Company, New York.

1. "Remember thy Creator in the days of thy youth." The word translated "youth" is the same Hebrew word translated "adolescence" in Hebrew writings. "The evil days" refers to the days of old age.

2. When the vision begins to fall, the sun, moon, and light grow dim. The earth is refreshed by the rain, but old age knows no renewal; the clouds return and continue to pile up.

3. The hands and the arms are the "keepers of the house." They begin to shake and tremble with age. Strong men become stooped. The grinders (teeth) cease because there aren't many of them. "And those that look out the windows be darkened," means eyesight is bad.

4. Psalm 141:3 refers to the lips as doors. The thought here in verse 4 is that the lips (doors) are wrinkled with streets. "The sound of the grinding is low," means the mouth is closed with wrinkles as he attempts to gum his food and not much chewing is heard.

   His voice is high pitched like a bird. This is typical of old age when the voice begins to tremble. "The daughters of music shall be brought low," means his voice is weak and low. This is typical of old age.

5. Fear of high places is known as acrophobia. This is a common fear in old age. Old age also brings more fears on level ground. The almond tree as described in botanical literature is generally pink; a few varieties are white. The pink blossoms fade to white with age. No doubt this turning to white refers to the hair turning white. Almond blossoms are described in at least one modern botany book as a hoary-headed old patriarch.

   "The grasshopper shall be a burden." Just to think of his muscle strength is too much. The grasshopper broad jumps about twenty times its body length. It can high jump about ten times its body length. If a 6-foot man were as efficient, he could broad jump 120 feet, and high jump sixty feet. The very thought of such muscle strength is a burden in old age.

   "And the caper-berry shall fail." The word translated "desire" in the King James is the word for caper berry. The young tender buds of the caper are pickled and used as a condiment. In some parts of the world, they are used as an appetite stimulant for the aged. In old age, even the caper berry fails to stimulate the appetite. "Desire" often is interpreted to mean sexual desire. This is not the thought conveyed by the use of the word *caper-berry*. The thought is that in old age, loss of appetite cannot be improved by the caper berry.

"His long home" refers to the grave. The Hebrew wording can mean cemetery. "The mourners go about the street," this may refer to professional mourners who are hired for funerals.

6. "The silver cord be loosed." This has reference to the cord that held the light in the temple. In this context, "the silver cord" refers to the spinal cord and vertebrae which are giving trouble in old age. "The golden bowl be broken" refers to the skull, and it implies that the individual is acting like a person with a fractured skull.

"The pitcher be broken at the fountain." It was customary to draw water with a pitcher. In a hot, dry country, water is the lifegiving substance. Likewise, the breath is the lifegiving substance that must be drawn. The lungs that draw the breath are not working properly in old age; shortness of breath occurs.

"The wheel at the cistern is broken." The wheel was used to pump water; this refers to the heart.

7. "Soon he will die." The body shall return to the dust and the spirit to God.

8. Empty of all emptiness.

"And the caper-berry shall fail" (Ecclesiastes 12:5).

The accompanying drawing is of the Mediterranean caper berry. The young, tender buds are pickled and used as an appetite stimulant. The buds are called caper berries; actually, they are caper buds because the berries are inedible.

Caper

Drawing by Alen Edgar, College Park, Md.

# IX

## GENETICS

"And every winged fowl after his kind: and God saw that it was good. And God made the beast of the earth after his kind, and cattle after their kind, and every thing that creepeth upon the earth after his kind: and God saw that it was good" (Genesis 1:21b, 25).

# 100

# Dwarfism

There are three basic types of dwarfism. *Pituitary* dwarfism is caused by improper functioning of the pituitary gland resulting in very small people who are mentally normal. People who have unusually small, well proportioned bodies are called *midgets*. Pituitary dwarfism rarely occurs today, because pituitary extracts can be given to prevent it. The *achondroplastic* (chondrodystrophic) dwarf is the result of a mutation. This trait is hereditary. This type of dwarf has very short legs and arms. His head is quite large and the trunk portion of the body may be normal. The third type of dwarf is a *cretin*. This condition results from an underactive thyroid during childhood. The individual remains the size of a small child and will be either mentally deficient or a total idiot. The cretin has poor coordination.

Leviticus 21:20 explains that a dwarf was not allowed to participate in the priestly service. Dwarfism is mentioned in a list of defects that disqualified one from becoming a Levitical priest. The significance of this passage is that the priest represented Christ, who is our Great High Priest. The Levitical priest had to be as near perfect as possible because he represented the perfect Man.

The priest was not able to offer the bread if he had a spot or blemish of any type; not just dwarfism, but a crookback, a broken foot, or a broken hand. In a similar manner, the sacrificial lamb had to be without spot or blemish. The blemish is a hereditary defect (symbolic of sin nature); whereas the spot is an acquired defect (symbolic of sins committed). The blemishes and defects represent imperfection; dwarfism is one of these many defects which symbolize imperfection.

The following verses illustrate why any type of defect disqualified a man from becoming a priest. Those in the earthly tabernacle symbolized Christ, our Great High Priest and His offering. Concerning Christ as priest, "For such an high priest became us, who is holy, harmless,

231

undefiled, separate from sinners, and made higher than the heavens; who needeth not daily, as those high priests, to offer up sacrifice, first for his own sins, then for the people's: for this he did once when he offered up himself" (Hebrews 7:26-27). "Forasmuch as ye know that ye were not redeemed with corruptible things, as silver and gold. . . . But with the precious blood of Christ, as a lamb without blemish and without spot" (1 Peter 1:18-19).

The fact that the priest could not have a broken bone was also a symbol of Christ. "Neither shall ye break a bone thereof" (Exodus 12:46). "But when they came to Jesus, and saw that he was already dead, they brake not his legs:

For these things were done, that the scripture should be fulfilled, a bone of him shall not be broken" (John 19:33, 36).

Drawing by Alen Edgar, College Park, Md.

## Dwarfism

Left to right: a cretin, an achondroplastic dwarf, and a midget.

Speak unto Aaron, saying, Whosoever he be of thy seed in their generations that hath any blemish, let him not approach to offer the bread of his God. For whatsoever man he be that hath a blemish, he shall not approach: a blind man, or a lame, or he that hath a flat nose, or anything superfluous, or a man that is brokenfooted, or brokenhanded, or crookbackt, or a dwarf, or that hath a blemish in his eye, or be scurvy, or scabbed, or hath his stones [testicles] broken; no man that hath a blemish of the seed of Aaron the priest shall come nigh to offer the offerings of the LORD made by fire; he hath a blemish; he shall not come nigh to offer the bread of his God. He shall eat the bread of his God. . . . Only he shall not go in unto the vail (Leviticus 21:17-23).

# 101

# Polydactylism

"And there was yet a battle in Gath, where was a man of great stature, that had on every hand six fingers and on every foot six toes, four and twenty in number; and he also was born to the giant" (2 Samuel 21:20).

Polydactylism is the condition of having more than the usual number of fingers or toes. The most common form in man results in six toes and six fingers on each foot and hand.

Polydactylism is hereditary and is due to a dominant gene. People with six fingers and six toes have offspring with an abnormal number.

Polydactylism is not restricted to man; it occurs in animals also. It has been reported in chickens and guinea pigs. Chickens normally have four toes, but occasionally one may have five. This condition can occur in any breed, but it has been reported in the Sumatra and White Plymouth Rock chickens.

Drawing by Alen Edgar, College Park, Md.

A six-fingered hand.

Polydactylism has been known since Bible times. It is mentioned in reference to war with the Philistines. In this particular reference it appears to be associated with giantism. This is a unique observation recorded in Scripture long before polydactylism became of interest. Information regarding polydactylism has been recorded in twentieth-century textbooks on genetics.

Photograph by Matson Photo Service, Alhambra, Calif.

### Valley of Elah.

According to 1 Samuel 17:2, David killed Goliath, the giant, in the Valley of Elah.

"And there went out a champion out of the camp of the Philistines, named Goliath, of Gath, whose height was six cubits and a span. . . . And it came to pass, when the Philistines arose, and came and drew nigh to meet David, that David hasted, and ran toward the army to meet the Philistine. And David put his hand in his bag, and took thence a stone, and slang it, and smote the Philistine in his forehead, that the stone sunk into his forehead; and he fell upon his face to the earth" (1 Samuel 17:4, 48-49).

# 102

# Giants

There are four different words translated "giant" in Scripture. In some cases it may be questionable whether "giant" is the exact meaning intended, but where sizes are quoted, the words refer to very large people. 1 Samuel 17:4 says Goliath of Gath was six cubits and a span tall. An ordinary cubit is 18 inches, and a span is 6 inches. This would mean that Goliath would be 9½ feet tall. In 1 Chronicles 11:23, Benaiah killed an Egyptian who was 5 cubits, or 7½ feet. Og, King of Bashan, slept in a bed that was 13½ feet long. This indicates he was a tall man.

In modern times, there are several who compare with the Bible account of giants. The giant Van Deusen was 8 feet 9 inches. Robert Madlow was 8 feet 8 inches; Eddie Carmal was advertized by a circus as being over 9 feet tall. Professional basketball players are frequently 7 feet tall, or taller.

True giantism is a result of excessive production of the growth hormone secreted by the pituitary gland. This hormone controls long bone development. True giantism is an abnormality. There are, however, normal individuals who are unusually tall because of an inherited trait. This is especially true of basketball players. A person who suffers from the pituitary disease generally has such poor coordination that he could not participate in sports.

In 2 Samuel 21:20, giantism is associated with polydactylism, a hereditary abnormality. This suggests the giantism may have been a hereditary abnormality rather than a pituitary problem.

# 103

# How Jacob Got Laban's Goat

The domesticated goat of the Holy Land was black (Song of Solomon 1:5). Some had white spots (Genesis 30:32). The goats had very long hair (Song of Solomon 4:1; 6:5). The goat's hair was woven into tents known as the tents of Kedar. The Bedouins still use these tents today, just as they did in ancient times.

In the Genesis record, Jacob agreed to take the goats that had white spots or streaks on them; Laban, Jacob's father-in-law, would keep the solid-colored ones (Genesis 30:32-33). This agreement must have pleased Laban because he must have known that the white spotted ones occurred in fewer numbers. White spotting is a recessive characteristic, and the ratio of solid to white spotting should be 3 to 1. Laban should have received three goats to Jacob's one. God intervened so that Jacob received more than normally expected.

The usual ratio may be seen in the following illustration. A solid-colored goat is mated with another solid-colored goat. Each goat carries the recessive gene for white spotting. If Ss is mated with Ss, the expected offspring, according to genetic principles, would be SS, Ss, Ss, and ss. SS, Ss, and Ss are solid colored; ss is spotted. This means that under ordinary circumstances, the most spotted offspring that could be expected from a union of two solid-colored goats is about one-fourth of the total offspring.

Jacob had placed spotted rods in front of the watering troughs. He may have been superstitious and believed that the spotted rods would cause the females to have white-spotted kids (Genesis 30:37-38). The rods would have no effect on the goats; the unborn are not affected by such external influences. God intervened so that Jacob's herd increased far beyond the expected ratio.

God intervened in several ways because the text says that Jacob's goats continued to increase (Genesis 31:8). He should have received only a few goats, but God increased the herd in his favor.

Dr. William J. Tinkle, in his comments on this passage, points out a very essential truth. He states that in a dream, God showed Jacob it was not his superstitious rods which caused solid females to give birth to spotted kids, but the fact that the females were being mated to rams (males) which carried genes for white spotting. "And the angel of God spake unto me in a dream, saying, Jacob: and I said, Here am I. And he said, Lift up now thine eyes, and see, all the rams which leap upon the cattle [goats] are ring-streaked, speckled, and grizzled: for I have seen all that Laban doeth unto thee" (Genesis 31:11-12).

Two scientific principles are illustrated here. First, the mother's experience during pregnancy does not affect the unborn. This was revealed to Jacob in a dream when God showed him what caused the females to bear white spotted kids. Second, there is a genetic rule that certain recessive traits may be transmitted to the offspring, even though the parent does not show that trait. This is called the heterozygous condition in genetics. These two scientific principles were not know to man until thousands of years later.

Photograph courtesy of Dack N. Patrick, Rockville, Md.

### Spotted goat

This goat is typical of those in the story of Jacob and Laban. Note the white spotting on the ears.

"I will pass through all thy flock today, removing from thence all the speckled and spotted cattle, and all the brown cattle among the sheep, and the spotted and speckled among the goats: and of such shall be my hire. And Laban said, Behold, I would it might be according to thy word. And he removed that day the he goats that were ringstraked and spotted, and all the she goats that were speckled and spotted, and every one that had some white in it, and all the brown among the sheep, and gave them into the hand of his sons" (Genesis 30:32, 34-35).

237

# 104

# Baldness

"And instead of well set hair baldness" (Isaiah 3:24b).

There are several kinds of baldness. Baldness may be caused by a thyroid condition, skin infection, nutritional deficiency, or heredity. Premature or pattern baldness in man is hereditary and appears to be a sex-limited trait. The work of J. B. Hamilton indicates there is a single dominant gene that causes this type of baldness. The gene for baldness is able to exert its influence when the male hormone (androgenic) reaches high enough level for expression. It is doubtful that the male hormone ever reaches high enough level in women to cause baldness. Baldness in women is related to other causes.

Baldness is spoken of in Ezekiel 29:18. This is often cited as an example of superstition in the Bible. This is an erroneous assumption because the people infer from this verse that baldness is a diseased condition. It states their shoulders were peeling. The children of Israel were not permitted to clip their heads bald because it represented a heathen practice. Natural baldness was acceptable. (See Leviticus 21:5.)

Children made fun of Elisha's bald head, and Elisha cursed them. It was not because of his bald head that it was such a serious offence, but it was near blasphemy to make fun of a servant of God. The children were merely using the bald head to make fun of the prophet of God. When Elisha cursed the children in the name of the Lord, he was not using profanity. He was calling down punishment upon them. It was not their attitude toward his bald head, their attitude toward a servant of God that was wrong, "And he [Elisha] went up thence unto Bethel and as he was going up by the way, there came forth little children out of the city, and mocked him, and said unto him, Go up thou bald head; go up thou bald head. And he turned back, and looked on them, and cursed them in the name of the LORD. And there came forth two she bears out of the wood, and tare forty and two children" (2 Kings 2:23-24).

## A team of mules threshing grain

This Middle East technique is about the same as it was in the time of King David.

"Ye shall keep my statutes. Thou shalt not let thy cattle gender with a diverse kind" (Leviticus 19:19).

# 105

# Breeding of Diverse Kinds

The breeding of diverse kinds was forbidden in Leviticus 19:19. This might apply to a cross between the jackass, *Equus asinus,* and a female horse, *Equus caballus,* which cross produces a mule. The mule is a sterile hybrid. When the opposite cross is made with a jenny (female donkey) and a stallion (male horse) the offspring is known as a hinny. The hinny is sterile. Crosses between the ass and zebra are also sterile. The forbiddance of breeding of diverse kinds was an extremely wise regulation for the time in which it was given. The build-up of a sterile herd of animals could be a disaster, especially if enough horses and asses were not maintained for future crosses.

Mules became very popular during King David's time. Perhaps by this time the problem of breeding them was understood. (See 2 Samuel 13:29 and 2 Samuel 18:9.)

Mules are stronger and have more endurance than either the horse or the donkey. They have small feet like the donkey, and this makes them more sturdy on their feet in rough terrain. The mule is distinguished from a horse by its large ears, short mane, small feet, and a tail with a tuft of long hair at the end. Mules are somewhat smaller than horses.

# X

# MEDICAL SCIENCES AND
# HEALTH PRACTICES

"Is there no balm in Gilead; is there no physician there?" (Jeremiah 8:22).

# 106

# Circumcision

"And when eight days were accomplished for the circumcising of the child, his name was called Jesus, which was so named of the angel before he was conceived in the womb" (Luke 2:21).

In 1935, H. Dam proposed the term *vitamin K* for a factor in foods which would prevent hemorrhaging in chicks. Vitamin K is known to be synthesized in the human intestinal tract by bacteria. Subsequently, vitamin K is responsible for synthesis of prothrombin by the liver. If vitamin K is deficient, there is a corresponding prothrombin deficiency and hemor-

Drawing by Alen Edgar, College Park, Md.

### Mary and Jesus

rhaging may occur. Since vitamin K is synthesized by bacteria in the intestinal tract, newborn infants are particularly disposed to suffer from vitamin K and prothrombin deficiencies. These deficiencies occur because newborn infants have not had time to become contaminated with bacteria.

Nathan Scanzillo has prepared a paper in which he indicates that the

243

rise of vitamin K and prothrombin levels in infants reaches its peak around the eighth day. Thus, he points out that circumcision is best performed on that day. Prothrombin levels rise to 30 percent on the third day of life, and to 110 percent the eighth; thereafter, it levels off to 100 percent. The eighth day is the best day to circumcise and avoid hemorrhaging.

"And Abraham circumcised his son Isaac being eight days old, as God had commanded him" (Genesis 21:4).

There are also some medical advantages in circumcision. Recent surveys show that gentile women have 8.5 percent times more cancer of the cervix than Jewish women. Careful studies indicate that the bacterium known as *Mycobacterium smegmatis* (smegma bacillus) inhabits the external genitourinary tract, but they tend to build up in the uncircumcised male. These bacteria can convey cancer of the cervix to women.

Circumcision is used in Scripture in the spiritual sense as well as in the physical sense. "Circumcise therefore the foreskin of your heart, and be no more stiffnecked" (Deuteronomy 10:16). "And the LORD thy God will circumcise thine heart, and the heart of thy seed, to love the LORD thy God with all thine heart, and with all thy soul, that thou mayest live" (Deuteronomy 30:6).

# 107

# Gangrene

To the right is a drawing of bacteria that cause gas gangrene. The cells may occur singly or in pairs. This was drawn from a prepared slide and is greatly enlarged.

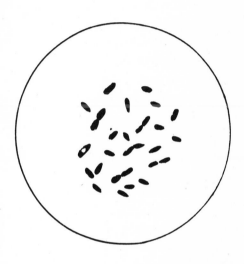

The word translated "canker" in 2 Timothy 2:17 is the Greek word *gaggarina*, meaning "gangrene." There are four common forms of gangrene: (1) gas gangrene, (2) diabetic gangrene, (3) senile gangrene, and (4) septic gangrene, which usually spreads from an ulcer or sore. The kind of gangrene that fits the description of 2 Timothy 2:17 is gas gangrene. "But shun profane and vain babblings: for they will increase unto more ungodliness. And their work will eat as doth a canker [*gaggarina*] of whom is Hymenaeus and Philetus: who concerning the truth have erred, saying that the resurrection is past already; and overthrow the faith of some" (2 Timothy 2:16-18).

There are three principal species of gangrene bacteria, but *Clostridium perfringens* is usually the predominating one. *Clostridia* ferment muscle sugar with a subsequent formation of gas bubbles in the infected tissue. The words "eat like gangrene," are appropriate because the bacteria spread rapidly. Rabbits experimentally injected with gangrene bacteria are completely taken over by the organisms in about twenty-four hours.

The use of the word gangrene is appropriate for this text in 2 Timothy because gangrene not only spreads rapidly, but it also causes the formation of gas bubbles so the tissues become puffed. In a similar manner, vain babblings will increase unto more ungodliness; the individual becomes puffed up.

# 108

# Boils

*Shechin* is the Hebrew word used for "boil" in 2 Kings 20:7, to describe Hezekiah's illness. This may have been an ordinary boil or furuncle. Boils or furuncles are acute skin infections caused by the bacterium *Staphylococcus aureus*. Some of the more virulent strains of Staphylococci may be fatal. If the bacteria are extremely potent, or if the individual's resistance is low,

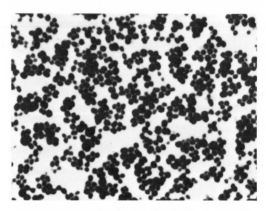

Courtesy of Turtox/Cambosco, MacMillan Science Co., Inc., Chicago, Ill.

Staphylococcus bacteria photomicrograph.

the patient may die suddenly of septicemia. Boils that form around the nose or lips may result in the bacteria gaining entrance into the membranes of the brain (the *dura mater*), and may subsequently involve the entire circulatory system. This may result in septicemia and finally death. Even in this modern age of antibiotics, resistant Staphylococcus outbreaks may produce many deaths.

Hezekiah's boil could have been one of several diseases. The use of the fig poultice, however, is an ancient remedy for boils, and is still used by some as a home remedy. If slightly green figs are eaten, they have a drawing effect on the tongue and the taste buds pop up fiery red. A fresh fig poultice has a drawing effect somewhat similar to the action of *ichthammol*. These were used for boils prior to the advent of antibiotics. The Hebrew *shechin* does not identify the illness, but the fig poultice suggests that it was a boil.

"In those days was Hezekiah sick unto death . . . . And Isaiah said, Take a lump of figs. And they took and laid it on the boil, and he recovered" (2 Kings 20:1*a*, 7).

# 109

# Gonorrhea

Gonorrhea is most likely the veneral disease described as a running issue, or discharge (Leviticus 15:2, 22:4-5; Numbers 5:2-3). According to *Gesenius Hebrew and Chaldee Lexicon*, the Hebrew word *zob* or *zub* may refer to gonorrhea discharge. The cleansing of the issue until evening does not imply a cure, but, rather, a method of hygiene. Gonorrhea is caused by a coccus-shaped bacterium known as *Neisseria gonorrhoeae.* It is transmitted by sexual contact. Man is the only natural host.

Veneral disease is the plague associated with Baalpeor worship. The words "joined himself" most likely makes reference to the pairing off of an Israelite and a Moabitess in some sort of worship involving sexual rites (Numbers 25:3).

The plague recorded in 1 Corinthians 10:8 surely seems to be venereal disease, but the particular type is not specified. It is perhaps both gonorrhea and syphilis. First Corinthians 10:8 records the number who died in one day, while Numbers 25:9 records the total number who died in the plague.

"Neither let us commit fornication, as some of them committed, and fell in one day three and twenty thousand" (1 Corinthians 10:8). "And Israel abode in Shittim, and the people began to commit whoredom with the daughters of Moab. And they called the people unto the sacrifice of their gods: and the people did eat, and bowed down to their gods. And Israel joined himself unto Baalpeor: and the anger of the LORD was kindled against Israel" (Numbers 25:1-3).

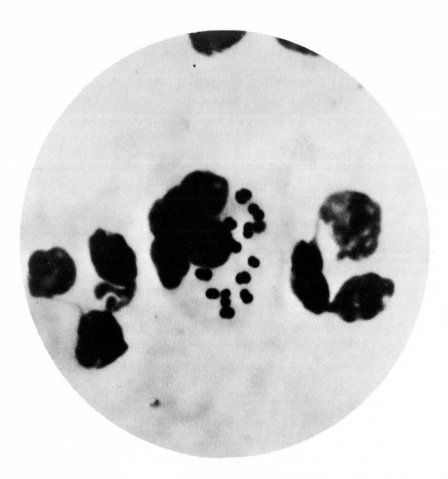

## Gonorrhea

"When any man hath a running issue" (Leviticus 15:2b).

This photomicrograph of *Neisseria gonorrhoeae* smears from exudate show the bacteria cells inside of white blood cells. The small black dots inside the cells are the bacteria. All other material belongs to the cell proper of the white blood cells. Only a faint outline of the white blood cells can be seen; the large dark spots are the nuclei of the white blood cells.

# 110

## Syphilis

Proverbs 7 describes a harlot who lures a man to her home. She tells him her husband is away on a long journey (vv. 18-19). She is trying to entice him to a delicious meal because the meat for the peace offering would be eaten that day (v. 14). She tells him in great detail how she has perfumed her bed with myrrh, aloes, and cinnamon, but fails to tell him she has venereal disease. Verse 23 seems to describe a person who has syphilis in the latter stages (tertiary syphilis). It states that a dart

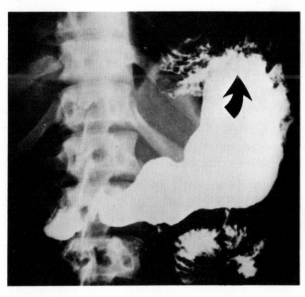

Photograph courtesy of the Armed Forces Institute of Pathology, Washington, D.C.

Syphilis invading the stomach.

or arrow strikes his liver, or, more literally, his vital organs. In the last stages, all the internal organs are subject to invasion; the brain, spinal cord, and nerves develop lesions which result in paresis, insanity, and finally death.

Syphilis is caused by a spiral shaped bacterium (spirochete) known as *Treponema pallidum.* The disease may be chronic for years, involving the vital organs in the last stage. Finally death occurs "And knoweth not that it is for his life" (Proverbs 7:23). Evidence indicates that the disease was once far more virulent and infectious, but after centuries it has become somewhat milder.

# 111

# Bubonic Plague

A plague broke out when the Philistines placed the ark of God in an idol's temple (1 Samuel 5:2,9,12). A description of the plague states they had tumors. The Hebrew *ophalin* means "mounds," not emerods or hemorrhoids as translated in the King James Version. Hemorrhoids are vericose veins of the anal region. They do no occur in epidemic form nor do they fit the description of *ophalin*. The mounds are said to occur in secret parts. The outbreak of plague was associated with mice (Hebrew *akhbar*) that mar the land (1 Samuel 6:5). *Akhbar* is also mentioned in Leviticus 11:29 with the unclean animals.

The plague mentioned in these references appears to be bubonic plague. This is transmitted by the bite of a rodent flea. The flea regurgitates a trace of bacteria whenever it bites its victim. The bubonic plague is caused by the bacterium, *Pasteurella pestis*. Bubos or mounds are formed in secret parts, the groins and armpits. "And they had emerods in their secret parts" (1 Samuel 5:9).

The Indian rat flea, *Xenopsylla cheopis*, is the principal vector of plague, and the rat is the principal host. The plague that swept the world during the Middle Ages was due to the Indian rat flea. More than one-fourth of the world's population died.

Bubonic plague is by no means limited to the rat; other rodents may be infected. Plague broke out in China in 1910, taking 60,000 lives. This was due to infected Manchurian marmots, animals important to the fur industry. In western United States, plague has been found in squirrels, chipmunks, prairie dogs, wood rats, and harvest mice. *Diamanus montanus*, the common flea of ground squirrels, has been reported to be infected. This is a potential danger, even though the animals live in the wild. Health authorities keep a close check on the field mice in western United States because field mice share winter quarters with rats. The disease could be shifted to man from wild animals at any time.

Experimental evidence indicates that almost any rodent can be infected with plague bacteria, and almost any flea can also be infected. The rat flea just happens to be more efficient in transmitting the disease, primarily because rats share man's quarters. Furthermore, it should be noted that whenever an infected rodent dies, the fleas will seek any host, including man.

There are three types of plague: (1) bubonic, (2) pneumonic, and (3) septicemic. Bubonic plague is transmitted by the bite of an infected flea. It is characterized by chills, fever, nausea, and the formation of bubos in the area of the lymph, the arm pits and groins. (This is most likely the meaning of the statement in 1 Samuel 5:9 regarding the mounds in secret parts.) Pneumonic plague is transmitted from person to person by airborne bacteria that enter the respiratory tract. The septicemic plague does not form bubos. (It was the septicemic form that gave the bubonic plague the name "black death." In this form, there are numerous hemorrhages under the skin that turn blackish.) The antibiotic, streptomycin, is effective against bubonic and pneumonic plague, provided it is administered in time.

In view of current findings that most any rodent can become infected with bubonic plague, it seems reasonable to suggest that this was most likely the plague of 1 Samuel 5:2; especially since the plague was associated with mice that mar the land (1 Samuel 6:5).

Photograph courtesy of the Armed Forces Institute of Pathology, Washington, D.C.

### Bubonic plague

A large bubos under the armpit of a man who has the bubonic plague.

# 112

# Anthrax

The murrain which broke out in cattle (Exodus 9:3) and in man (Exodus 9:9) during the Egyptian captivity may have been anthrax. Anthrax is a disease which attacks cattle, sheep, goats, and horses; man can become infected. The disease is caused by a rod-shaped bacterium known as *Bacillus anthracis.* This bacterium forms very resistant spores that may contaminate the hair of animals, forage, and dust. The spores are extremely virulent and remain alive for many years in dust or wool. It is interesting to note that in Exodus 9:5, the disease was to strike tomorrow. The incubation period for anthrax is approximately twenty-four hours. In Exodus 9:3, the plague is apparently limited to cattle in the field, but in 9:9 it includes both man and cattle throughout Egypt. Exodus 9:3 indicates the plague was a grievous murrain; the Targum Of Jonathan renders it "death." Anthrax is usually fatal.

Human anthrax is contracted from animals or animal products that contain the spores. It is sometimes called woolsorter's disease because the spores get into the fleece and infect a person who sorts wool. In humans, the disease produces a boil-like lesion with a pustule (blain). In the infective stage, the blain is called a malignant pustule. The use of the word *malignant* should not confuse this disease with cancer.

Ordinary boils do not fit the picture described in Exodus 9. Ordinary boils do not occur in epidemic form, nor do they simultaneously infect cattle. Some authors have suggested that smallpox was involved in the fifth and sixth plagues in Exodus. This does not seem to fit the description because the poxes are all different, viral diseases. Cowpox is a very mild disease; smallpox is very severe. Furthermore, smallpox requires about a twelve-day incubation period.

The smallpox (*variola*) and cowpox (*vaccinia*) viruses are similar enough to stimulate antibody production. During early times it was noted that milkmaids who had had cowpox did not contract smallpox. This is the basis of the smallpox vaccination. Cowpox is so mild that it could scarcely be considered a plague.

Animals suffering from anthrax generally have the acute form. They suddenly become ill, stagger, breathe with difficulty, and finally go into convulsions. The Exodus plague indicates that there were boil-like lesions.

There is a cutaneous form of anthrax in animals, but this is not the common pathway for the disease. The cutaneous form in animals is characterized by swellings which occur following bites by flies or some sort of skin abrasions. It seems possible the cutaneous form could have occurred following the plague of flies (Exodus 8:24). The description of the disease in Exodus could be the cutaneous form of anthrax, but not the acute form in animals. (Compare the description of anthrax by Stein and Van Ness in the *Yearbook of Agriculture, 1956*.)

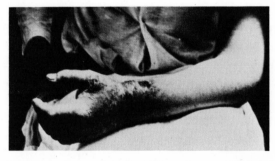

The infection has spread throughout her arm so that it is difficult to see the original pustules.

"And it shall become dust in all the land of Egypt, and shall be a boil breaking forth with blains upon man, and upon beast, throughout all the land of Egypt" (Exodus 9:9).

Photograph courtesy of the Armed Forces Institute of Pathology, Washington, D. C.

A woman infected with anthrax

# 113

# Leprosy, or Hanson's Disease

Three diseases are known as leprosy. True leprosy is Hanson's disease. It is caused by a rod-shaped bacterium, *Mycobaterium leprae.* There are two manifestations of Hanson's disease: the lepromatous and the tuberculoid. The lepromatous type begins with reddish spots on the arms and face. These spots thicken into nodules, then the nodules lose skin and become ulcerated. The tuberculoid type is characterized by atrophy of the muscles and nerves: the affected part becomes numb. It is this manifestation of leprosy that causes maiming and crippling.

The second disease that is known as leprosy, although it is not true leprosy, is elephantiasis, or black leprosy. It should be referred to as elephantiasis, the general medical name, to avoid confusing it with Hanson's disease. Elephantiasis is characterized by edema and is caused by worms.

The other disease misnamed leprosy is found in India. It is called white leprosy. Its general medical name is leucoderma, and this disease causes loss of skin pigmentation.

True leprosy, or Hanson's disease, was present in the Orient and India by at least 1500 B.C. and is present today. It was not known in ancient Greece, and the term *leprosy* was greatly confused because of the difference in Greek and Oriental terminology. The Greeks and the Romans called elephantiasis *leprosy.* Aretaeus described leontiasis under the name *leprosy.* The Greeks described psoriasis under the term *lepra.* (See the *Origin of Medical Terms* by H. A. Skinner.)

Leprosy was more apt to be contracted in ancient times because of unsanitary conditions. Although this fact is often disputed, the number of cases of leprosy among the poor seems to verify it. In addition, the lepromatous type is known to be contagious, but it is doubtful whether the tuberculoid type is contagious. By the time the symptoms develop, it does not appear to be spreading live bacteria.

During the twelfth century, there were thousands of leper houses in Germany and France. In ancient times, the lepromatous type was the more common form; today the tuberculoid tends to be most common in certain parts of the world.

Leprosy was dreaded in ancient times because the disease was incurable, and the leper became a social outcast. The disease as we know it today is not highly contagious. It can be arrested by sulfone drugs and the use of certain antibiotics. Modern navy manuals recommend isolation for people with the lepromatous type of leprosy. Leprosy bacilli are transmitted from infected skin, nasal drippings, and saliva. The disease can be passed only through close, personal contact. Leper colony workers frequently do not believe that lepers should be isolated.

Leviticus 13 outlines the procedure for isolating a patient with leprosy. If only the epidermis was infected, the disease had to be watched carefully for pathological changes and the patient isolated for seven days (Leviticus 13:4). If the disease had penetrated into the skin, the dermal layer, and caused changes in the hair, leprosy was suspected and the individual diagnosed as unclean. Ordinary skin infections scab over in two weeks (Leviticus 13:5-6). Raw flesh signifies infection or leprosy; scabs mean the skin is healing and not leprous (Leviticus 13:6, 14).

In Scripture, the term *leprosy* is applied to several skin diseases. The Hebrew term for leprosy, *zara'at*, identified both contagious and noncontagious skin diseases. (The Hebrew word was also used to designate contaminated houses and clothes, Leviticus 13:47; 14:34.) Those cases of leprosy requiring permanent isolation mentioned in Scripture appear to be cases of true leprosy, Hanson's disease. The four lepers who were compelled to live outside Samaria appear to be true lepers (2 Kings 7:3-10). King Uzziah was also isolated in separate quarters and was never cured of the disease. Leviticus required lepers to cover their upper lips and cry "Unclean!" Since the leprosy bacilli are transmitted from nasal drippings and saliva, this practice of having lepers cover their upper lips was a good hygienic policy.

Many writers refuse to acknowledge that biblical leprosy was the true leprosy, Hanson's disease. This is mainly because biblical leprosy was said to be cured, whereas true leprosy is merely arrested. Another reason these writers do no accept Hanson's disease as the biblical leprosy is that no leprosy victims have been found in tombs. The tuberculoid type of leprosy is the crippler. The lepromatous type, which is the type of leprosy described in Scripture, does not cripple. The lepromatous type progresses much faster than the tuberculoid, particularly in the early stages. The crippling tuberculoid type takes years to bring about the degeneration of muscles and nerve tissue. Since leprosy was known in the first Christian era but no evidence of the crippling leprosy has been found in the tombs, the idea that the lepromatous type of leprosy was the biblical leprosy is further supported.

The Scripture indicates that Jesus upheld every detail of the Mosaic regulations when He sent the cured leper to see the priest to have him remove the quarantine (Matthew 8:1-4). Scripture further indicates that leprosy and its subsequent isolation was an illustration of our sin that separates us from God. As must true lepers, the sinner must accept God's divine cure. "And he said unto him, Arise, go thy way: thy faith hath made thee whole" (Luke 17:19).

This modern day leper hides in the shadows of the streets of Jerusalem. He has the tuberculoid type of true bacterial leprosy. Note stubs for hands.

"And as he [Jesus] entered into a certain village, there met him ten men that were lepers, which stood afar off: and they lifted up their voices, and said, Jesus, Master, have mercy on us. And when he saw them, he said unto them, Go show yourselves unto the priests. And it came to pass, that, as they went, they were cleansed" (Luke 17:12-14).

Photograph by Wolfe Worldwide Films, Los Angeles, Calif.

A Leper

256

# 114

# Elephantiasis

It is doubtful that elephantiasis is a biblical disease. It is discussed here only because it is often confused with true leprosy. Elephantiasis is generally called filariasis or wuchereriasis in medical literature. In Christian literature and commentaries, it is called black leprosy. Because it is called black leprosy, it has been confused with true bacterial leprosy, or Hanson's disease.

Elephantiasis is caused by a parasitic round worm; the disease is transmitted to humans by the mosquito. The mosquito transmits minute infective larvae to the human host through the bite. Symptoms usually do not occur until the individual has had the disease many years. It is rarely found in persons under thirty years of age. In order for the symptoms to be exhibited, several re-infections over an extremely long period of time are necessary.

The disease is characterized by blockage of the lymphatics, primarily affecting the legs and genitalia. Blockage of the lymph system by the adult worms is accompanied by abnormal proliferation of connective tissues, excessive edema, and secondary bacterial infection. The legs become abnormally large like an elephant's. A darkening of the tissues, especially in the leg regions, gives it the common name of black leprosy.

Elephantiasis bears no relationship to true leprosy. Furthermore, it bears no relationship to the disease described in Scripture under the name of leprosy. The principal characteristic of elephantiasis is edema. The word *edema* (dropsy) occurs in Luke 14:2, but no clues are given to the nature of the disease. It may be caused by other diseases, such as a kidney ailment or poor circulation.

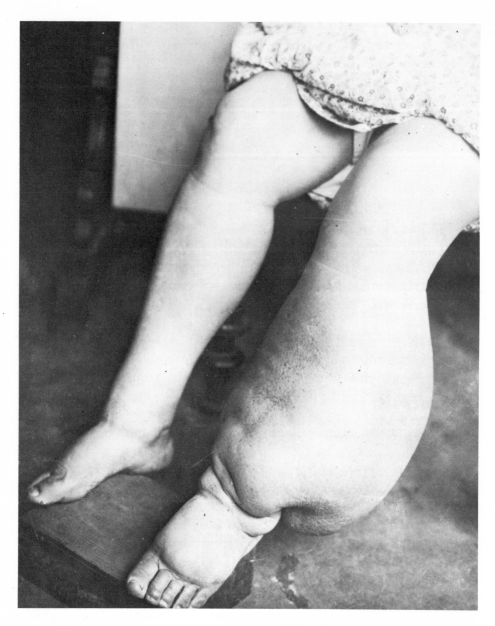

Photograph courtesy of the Armed Forces Institute of Pathology, Washington, D. C.

## Elephantiasis

A typical case of elephantiasis is characterized by edema, especially in the leg regions. The disease is not related to leprosy, or Hanson's disease described in Leviticus 13.

258

# 115

# Bagdad Boil

Bagdad boil may well have been Job's affliction. This type of boil goes by various names, such as oriental sore, Aleppo button, and cutaneous Leishmania. The incidence of Bagdad boil is high in the Middle East, particularly in the Dead Sea area of Jordan. The disease is produced by a protozoan parasite that is transmitted to man by the bite of sandflies that belong to the genus *Phlebotomus*. There are two general types of the disease, a wet type known as *Leishmania tropica var major* and a dry type known as *Leishmania tropica var minor*. The wet type generally produces multiple lesions, whereas the dry type rarely produces more than one lesion. In acute infections of the wet type, as many as one hundred or more boil-like lesions have been reported. Simultaneous infection by both types has also been reported.

*Leishmania* can infect the mucous membranes of the mouth, nose, and throat as well as the skin. These lesions may cause scarring and mutilation to the extent that it is difficult to recognize a person. The disfigurement of the victim also is similar to Job's experience. "And when they lifted up their eyes afar off, and knew him not" (Job 2:12).

The wet type of the disease may manifest itself in about two weeks by boil-like lesions that are at first glazed purple in appearance. Later the nodules become covered with dark, crusty scales. They itch intensely at this stage. Job sat in the ashes and soot, scraping off the scales with a potsherd (a piece of broken pottery). The potsherd would not be needed if these were ordinary boils.

"So went Satan forth from the presence of the LORD, and smote Job with sore boils from the sole of his foot unto his crown. And he took him a potsherd to scrape himself withal; and he sat down among the ashes" (Job 2:7-8).

As the disease progressed, the nodules turned into ulcers and oozed pus. At this stage, flies laid their eggs in his sores (ulcers), and the eggs had hatched into maggots. The text in Job 7:5 indicates these are maggots by the use of the word *rimman*. There are several flies that lay their eggs in wounds. The maggots that hatch in the wound also decompose carcasses. The use of the Hebrew word *rimman* in Job 24:20 indicates this is a decomposition maggot. "The worm shall feed sweetly on him" (Job 24:20).

A large number of the commentaries attribute Job's illness to a disease known as elephantiasis. This does not seem likely because elephantiasis does not fit the description of Job's disease. The text of Job indicates he was smitten with (Hebrew *shechin*) boils. The lymphatic invasion by elephantiasis does not look like a boil. It does have nodular swellings produced by blockage from the adult worms, but these do not resemble a boil.

If elephantiasis were Job's illness, the potsherd would be of little help. The skin does not generally become dry and flaky until years after repeated infection and after circulation has been impaired. The suggestion that Job's illness was elephantiasis is based on the idea that Job 30:30 states that his skin was black. But it should be noted that Job is sitting among the ashes and soot and this may account for his black skin.

Furthermore, the scales produced by Bagdad boil are dirty and dark looking. It seems reasonable to suggest that Bagdad boil may have been Job's affliction.

In spite of Job's calamity he has this to say: "For I know that my redeemer liveth, and that he shall stand at the latter day upon the earth: and though after my skin worms destroy this body, yet in my flesh shall I see God: whom I shall see for myself, and mine eyes shall behold, and not another; though my reins be consumed within me" (Job 19:25-27).

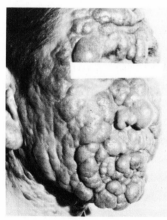

Photograph courtesy of the Armed Forces Institute of Pathology, Washington, D. C.

*Cutaneous Leishmania,* a very severe case.

# 116

# Eaten of Worms

The account of Herod Agrippa's death is recorded in Acts 12:21-23. Josephus records the set day as a festive occasion honoring the Emperor Claudius (Ant. XIX:8,2). Josephus also described Herod's royal apparel, a robe made of silver. "And upon a set day Herod, arrayed in royal apparel, sat upon his throne, and made an oration unto them. And the people gave a shout, saying, It is the voice of a god, and not of a man. And immediately an angel of the Lord smote him, because he gave not God the glory: and he was eaten of worms, and gave up the ghost" (Acts 12:21-23).

The phrase, "eaten of worms," in Greek is *skolakobrotos.* The root word *skolax,* means "a specific head structure of a tapeworm." Since the word *scolex* (plural *scolices*) is applied to the head of tapeworms, Herod's death was almost certainly due to the rupture of a cyst formed by a tapeworm. There are several kinds of tapeworms, but one of the most common ones found in sheep-growing countries is the dog tape, *Echinococcus granulosus.* The heaviest infections come from areas where sheep and cattle are raised. Sheep and cattle serve as intermediate hosts for the parasite. The dog eats the infected meat, then man gets the eggs from the dog, usually by fecal contamination of hair.

The disease is characterized by the formation of cysts, generally on the right lobe of the liver; these may extend down into the abdominal cavity. The rupture of such a cyst may release as many as two million scolices. The developing worms inside of the cysts are called scolices, because the anterior region constitutes the major part of development at this stage. When the cyst ruptures, the entrance of cellular debris along with the scolices may cause sudden death.

The use of the word *scolex* is not limited to this reference about Herod;

the term also appears in Mark 9:44. A literal translation of the phrase in Mark 9:44 would read, "where their scolex dieth not." This usage is very interesting because the tapeworm keeps propagating itself. Each section of the worm is a self-contained unit which has both male and female parts. The posterior part matures and forms hundreds of worm eggs. The word *scolex* in this text portrays a biological description of permanence which the text demands for the comparison. The text is rendered "maggot" in most translations; however, a maggot is an intermediate larval stage in the development of a fly, and is only temporary. The word *scolex* as given in the Greek conveys the idea of permanence which the text implies.

Photograph courtesy of The Armed Forces Institute of Pathology, Washington, D. C.

## Tapeworm cyst

This cyst of the dog tapeworm which was removed from the liver. The cyst has been cut in half; it contains millions of minute scolices.

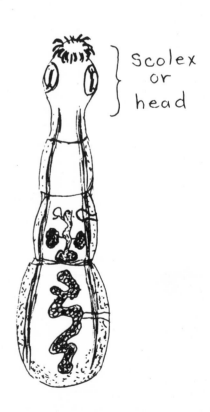

Adult tapeworm

# 117

# Dysentery

The Greek word *dusenteria*, (dysentery) used in Acts 28:8 to describe the fever that the father of Publius had was perhaps *shigellosis* dysentery. The term *dysentery* means an illness characterized by diarrhea. There are several dysentery organisms, but the principal species is *Shigella dysenteriae*. This bacterium produces a strong toxin which may inflame the intestional tract causing the characteristic

Bacteria that cause shigellosis

bloody stools or bloody flux. This is perhaps what prompted the translators to translate *dusenteria* as bloody flux.

Some authors have suggested cholera for this dysentery. Asiatic cholera was confined to the Delta of the Ganges River in India for nearly 2,000 years after its first mention in written history. It wasn't until the Portuguese navigator, Vasco da Gama, discovered the sea route to India that cholera broke out into an epidemic throughout the world. (See *Disease and History* by Frederick Cartwright.) Cholera is endemic along the Ganges River and from there severe epidemics have swept over most of the world. The limited geographical distribution of cholera seems to eliminate it as a possibility for Publius's fever.

Amoebic dysentery has been suggested as Publius's fever, but this does not seem likely because it tends to be chronic rather than acute. The outright clinical symptoms develop in about 10 percent of infected individuals. It tends to run a subacute course over a long period of time. Publius's fever appears to have been an acute attack, most likely that of bacillary dysentery known as shigellosis.

# 118

# The Seven-Year Itch

The Hebrew word *garab* has been identified by the Jerusalem Biblical Zoo as pertaining to the itch mite, *Sarcoptes scabiei. Garab* is translated "scab" in Deuteronomy 28:27, and "scurvy" in Leviticus 21:20 and 22:22. Several references in the Targums also identify this word as pertaining to the seven-year itch.

The itch is caused by a mite that burrows into the skin, making a tunnel in which the female lays her eggs. The short development causes the disease to spread rapidly.

The itch usually starts between the fingers, then spreads to other selected parts of the body. The presence of the disease may be determined by removing a mite from its tunnel with the aid of a needle. Other methods are not reliable.

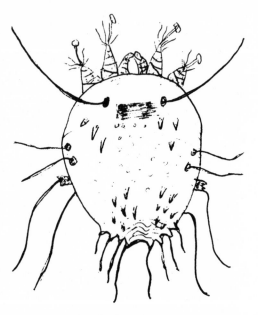

An itch mite

According to Deuteronomy 28:27, the Lord would smite the children of Israel with itch. In Leviticus 21:20 and 22:22, the Hebrew word *garab* has been mistranslated "scurvy." Scurvy could not be the disease. It is due to a vitamin C deficiency and is a very slow disease. The symptoms appear only after a prolonged deficiency. According to Deuteronomy 28:27, the chastening of the Lord would result in the seven-year itch.

# 119

# Dead Bodies, a Source of Diseases

Puerperal fever (childbirth fever) is due to an infection caused by the bacterium *Streptococcus pyrogenes*. Other organisms may be involved, but the principal causitive agent is *Streptococcus*. Childbirth fever or puerperal fever bacteria are introduced from external sources by the doctor or midwife. In a few rare cases the bacteria could be present in the birth canal, but for the most part, the infection is due to external contamination.

Oliver Wendell Homes, a physician and writer, was one of the first to insist that puerperal fever was contagious. He wrote "The Contagiousness of Puerperal Fever." Ignaz Philipp Semmelweis was one of the first to notice that childbirth fever occurred in patients who were attended by students of anatomy who went directly from the autopsy room to the maternity ward. The disease was being carried directly from the dead bodies to the mothers in the maternity ward. The views of Semmelweis were never widely accepted. As a part of his efforts against childbirth fever, he published "The Cause, Concept, and Prophylaxis of Childbed Fever." Successful antiseptic surgical techniques were not adopted until the work of Joseph Lister. Lister recommended the use of carbolic acid solutions as a disinfectant for surgical materials.

Thousands of years before Semmelweis suggested that dead bodies were the source of infection, the Scripture warned against touching dead bodies.

> He that toucheth the dead body of any man shall be unclean seven days. This is the law, when a man dieth in a tent: all that come into the tent, and all that is in the tent, shall be unclean seven days. And whosoever toucheth one that is slain with a sword in the open fields, or a dead body, or a bone of a man, or a grave, shall be unclean seven days (Numbers 19:11, 14, 16).

Pork tapeworm—Some infected pork has larval cysts in the meat. When man ingests these cysts, the small worms are freed from the cysts by digestive juices. The worms attach to the intestine and absorb nutrients through their body wall. The adult worm grows to about ten to twelve feet long. The name of the pork tapeworm is *Taenia solium.* Man may be infected by two different forms of this pork tapeworm, depending on whether eggs or larval cysts are ingested. Man may serve as an intermediate host or as a definitive host for this parasite.

Cysticercus—If eggs of the pork tapeworm are ingested, cysts instead of the adult worms develop in man. They may form in striated muscles, *pia mater* of the brain, and various subcutaneous tissues. It is ten to twenty years before this slow disease becomes fatal. The accompanying drawing shows cysticercus after it was removed from encysted muscle.

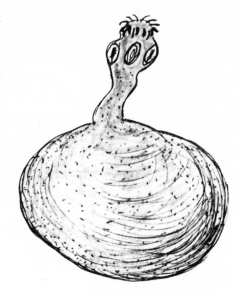

Pork tapeworm

This drawing of a pork tapeworm was made from a prepared slide of a whole mount of the worm.

The health regulations set forth in Leviticus are extremely advanced. They reveal God's divine care for his people.

# 120

# Diseases Caused by Swine

"And the swine, though he divide the hoof, and be clovenfooted, yet he cheweth not the cud; he is unclean to you. Of their flesh shall ye not eat, and their carcass shall ye not touch; they are unclean to you" (Leviticus 11:7-8).

The forbidding of swine as food is perhaps one of the most important health regulations set forth in the Bible. This was a very important regulation because of lack of refrigeration and that roasting pork over an open flame is not adequate to destroy parasites. It is also remarkable that they are told not to touch the carcass since these parasites are now known to be obtained by handling fresh pork.

Diseases are commonly caused by eating infected pork that is improperly cooked. These diseases still occur even in modern times with all the fancy equipment for cooking.

One of the more common of these diseases is trichinosis. When man ingests infected pork with the *Trichinella* larvae, the capsule surrounding each larva is dissolved by the digestive juices and the larva attaches to the intestine. From there, they may enter the blood stream by boring through the intestine, or the female may deposit them directly

Drawing of a cyst as it appears in infected pork.

into the blood stream or lymph. Larvae are carried to all parts of the body, but they are capable of development only in striated muscle. The parasite that causes trichinosis is *Trichinella spiralis*.

# 121

# Shellfish

The dietary instructions in Leviticus 11:10-11 state that fish with scales and fins may be eaten, but all seafood lacking scales and fins are forbidden. Such a dietary regulation automatically forbids shellfish such as clams, oysters, mussels, and crabs. These are forbidden not only as food, but the carcasses are to be an abomination. Such regulations indicate health standards far beyond what would have been expected at such a time; they suggest God's loving care for his people.

Shellfish such as oysters, mussels, clams, and crabs grow in fecal-contaminated waters. They are sometimes contaminated with enteric organisms which cause typhoid fever, paratyphoid fever, dysentery, and other diseases. The degree of contamination is dependent upon the degree of pollution. Some organisms tend to be a little more selective for pollutants than others. Mussels have been reported to have rather high rates of infectivity from sewage pollution. These may cause intestinal disturbances, paralysis, and death. Such advanced health regulations give evi-

dence that these were God-given and support divine inspiration of the Scriptures. "And all that have not fins and scales in the seas, and in the rivers, of all that move in the waters, and of any living thing which is in the waters, they shall be an abomination unto you; they shall be even an abomination unto you; ye shall not eat of their flesh, but ye shall have their carcasses in abomination" (Leviticus 11:10-11).


O the depth of the riches
      both of the wisdom and knowledge of God!
      how unsearchable are his judgments, and
      his ways past finding out!
For who hath known the mind of the Lord?
      or who hath been his counsellor?
For by him [Christ] were all things created,
      that are in heaven, and that are in earth,
      visible and invisible, whether they be thrones,
      or dominions, or principalities, or powers:
      all things were created by him, and for him:
And he is before all things,
      and by him all things consist [are held together].
All things were made by him; and without him was
      not any thing made that was made.
Thou art worthy, O Lord, to receive glory and
      honour and power: for thou hast created all
      things, and for thy pleasure they are and
      were created.
      (Romans 11:33-34, Colossians 1:16-17
      John 1:3, Revelation 4:11)

# Selected Bibliography

## BIBLES

*The Amplified Bible.* Grand Rapids: Zondervan Publishing House, 1971.

Harkavy, Alexander. *The Pentateuch with Haphtaroth and Five Megiloth.* New York: The Hebrew Publishing House, 1966.

Hirsch, Samson Raphael. *The Pentateuch and Haphtaroth.* London: Issac Levy, 1963.

*The Holy Bible, American Standard Version.* New York: Thomas Nelson and Sons, 1901.

*The Holy Bible, King James Version.* New York: Regency Publishing House, 1973.

Lamsa, George, trans. *The Holy Bible from the Peshitta Manuscripts.* Philadelphia: Holman Publishers, 1957.

*La Sainte Bible.* qui comprend l'ancien et le ouveau Testament traduits d'apres les texts originaux Hebrew et Grec par Louis Segon. Paris, 1965.

Rosenbaum, M., et al. *The Pentateuch with Targum Onkelos, Haphtaroth and Rashi's Commentary.* five vols. New York: The Hebrew Publishing Company, nd.

## GENERAL REFERENCE WORKS

*Book of Popular Science.* vol. 8. New York: Grolier, Inc., 1969.

*Encyclopedia Judaica.* 16 vols. New York: MacMillan Company, 1971.

Even-Shoshan, A. *HA-Millon HE-Chadesh,* 3 vols. (The New Dictionary.) Jerusalem: Kyrat-Sepher Publishers, 1975.

Fairbridge, Rhodes, W., ed. *Encyclopedia of Oceanography.* New York: Reinhold Publishing Corp., 1966.

*Grzimek's Animal Life Encyclopedia.* vol. 12. New York: Van Nostrand Reinhold, 1975.

*The Jewish Encyclopedia.* 12 vols. New York: Ktav Publishing House, Inc., 1901.

Kittel, Gerhard. *Theological Dictionary of the New Testament.* Edited by Geoffrey Bromiley. Grand Rapids: William B. Eerdmans Publishing Co., 1964

*Larousse Encyclopedia of Astronomy.* London: Hamlyn Lts., 1968.

Morris, Desmond. *Handbook of Mammals.* London: Zoological Society of London, 1965.

Pfeiffer, Charles F. *Baker's Bible Atlas*. Grand Rapids: Baker Book House, 1973.

Tregelles, Samuel. *Gesenius Hebrew and Chaldee Lexicon to the Old Testament*. Grand Rapids: William B. Eerdmans Publishing Co., 1957.

## TECHNICAL REFERENCES

Bentley, W. A.; Humphreys, W. J. *Snow Crystals*. New York: Dover Publications, Inc., 1931.

Breland, Osmond. *Animal Life and Lore*. New York: Harper and Row, 1972.

Bullinger, Ethelbert W. *Witness of the Stars*. Grand Rapids: Kregel Publishers, 1967.

Cartwright, Frederick F.; Biddiss, Michael. *Disease and History*. New York: Thomas Y. Crowell Co., 1972.

Charles, R. H., ed. *The Apocrypha and Pseudepigraphs of the Old Testament*. vols. I, II. Oxford: Oxford Clarendon Press, 1969.

Elazari-Volcani, Benjamin. *Studies of the Microflora of the Dead Sea*. Jerusalem: The Hebrew University, 1940.

Engel, Leonard; et. al. *The Sea*. New York: Time, Inc., 1963.

Epstein, I. *The Babylonian Talmud, Seder Nashim, Mo'ed Nezikin, Kodashim*. London: Soncino Press, 1964.

Griffin, A. ed. *The Talmud, Midrashim, and Kabbala*. London: M. Walter Dunne Publishers, 1901.

Grossfeld, Bernard. ed. *The Targum to the Five Megilloth*. New York: Hermon Press, 1973.

Guggisberg, C. A. W. *Simba, the Life of the Lion*. Philadelphia: Chilton Books, 1963.

Holmes, Capt. David C., USN. *Weather Made Clear*. New York: Sterling Publishing Co., 1965.

Idyll, C. P., ed. *Exploring the Ocean World, A History of Oceanography*. New York: Thomas Y. Crowell, 1969.

Lewis, Charles L. *Matthew Fontaine Maury, Pathfinder of the Sea*. Annapolis: U.S. Naval Institute, 1927.

Naval Bureau of Medicine and Surgery, *Poisonous Snakes of the World*. Washington D. C.: The Government Printing Office, 1962.

Rimmer, Harry. *The Lawsuit Against the Bible*. Grand Rapids: William B. Eerdmans Publishing Co., 1940.

Robertson, A. T. *Word Pictures in the New Testament*. Nashville: Broadman Press, 1930.

Shulov, A. *List of the Animals Mentioned in the Bible*. Jerusalem: The Jerusalem Biblical Zoological Gardens, Ltd., 1975.

Skinner, H. A. *Origin of Medical Terms*. Baltimore: Williams and Wilkins Company, 1961.

Tinkle, William. *Heredity.* Grand Rapids: Zondervan Publishing Co., 1970.

Whitcomb, John C. and Morris, Henry M. *The Genesis Flood.* Philadelphia: Presbyterian and Reformed Publishing Co., 1961.

Woods, Andrew J. *The Center of the Earth.* San Diego: Institute for Creation Research, 1974.

Wood, Gerald, *Animal Facts and Feats.* New York: Doubleday and Co., Inc. 1972.

## ARTICLES

Heezen, B. C. and Hollister, C. D. "Deep Sea Current Evidence from Abyssal Sediments." *Marine Geology.* 1964, 1, 141-174.

Menard, H. W. "Deepsea Channels, Topography, and Sedimentation." *Bull. Am. Assoc. Petrol. Geologists.* 1955, 39:236-255.

Scanzillo, Nathan. *Essay on Circumcision.* (Unpublished Term Paper). 1975.

Stein, C. D. and Van Ness, G. B. "Anthrax." *Yearbook of Agriculture.* Washington, D. C.: Government Printing Office, 1956.

Wust, G. "Stromgeschwindigkeiten im Tiefenund Bodenwasser des Atlantichen Ozeans" *Deepsea Research.* 1955, 3(Suppl.) 373-397.

U. S. Congress. House. *Hearing on Atmosphere—Committee on Science and Technology.* Ninety-Fourth Congress, 2nd Sess., 1976.